THE SECRET OF LIGHT

THE SECRET OF LIGHT

By

WALTER RUSSELL

UNIVERSITY OF SCIENCE AND PHILOSOPHY
FORMERLY THE WALTER RUSSELL FOUNOATION
SWANNANOA, WAYNESBORO, VIRGINIA 22980

KALPAZ

ISBN: 978-93-5128-919-7

First Published in 1947

Indian Reprint in 2017

Published by

Kalpaz Publications
C-30, Satyawati Nagar,
Delhi – 110052
Ph.: 011-47034999, 9811692060
www.kalpazpublications.com
E-mail: kalpaz@hotmail.com

Printed at: Gyan Press, Delhi.

Cataloging in Publication Data—DK
Courtesy: D.K. Agencies (P) Ltd. <docinfo@dkagencies.com>

Russell, Walter, 1871-1963, **author.**
The secret of light / by Walter Russell.
pages cm
Reprint. Originally published: Swannanoa, Va. : University of Science and Philosophy, 1947.
ISBN 9789351289197 (HB)

1. Occultism. I. Title.

BF1999.R886 2017 DDC 130 23

PREFACE TO 1971 EDITION

The original volume of THE SECRET OF LIGHT was published in 1947. This current publication includes some modifications and amplifications that Doctor Russell made with regard to this particular volume prior to his refolding in 1963.

Since THE SECRET OF LIGHT was released by Walter Russell, our year's Home Study Course in Universal Law, Natural Science and Living Philosophy—and all of the other books listed herein—have been written and released, for the world is now fully ready and in great need of the new and basic knowledge contained in all of these writings.

LAO RUSSELL

CONCERNING THE DIVINE ILIAD

THE DIVINE ILIAD *is the basis of this book.* THE DIVINE ILIAD *is an inspired message from the Creator to give man the needed comprehension of his relation to his universe, to man, and to God, for the coming cycle.*

Man progresses in cycles of approximately twenty-five hundred years. At the beginning of each cycle of his growing awareness of the Light within him, God sends messages through prepared messengers to further his comprehension of the Light. Comprehension of these cosmic messages gradually exalts mankind into higher beings, and thus each cycle is one more step for man toward full awareness of the Light, and of his Oneness with God.

THE DIVINE ILIAD *cannot be fully published for many years. As much of it as can now be published will appear in these pages. Further portions of it will be released as the world is ready to receive them.*

WALTER RUSSELL

PREFACE TO 1994 EDITION

This 1994 edition of Walter Russell's classic masterpiece has been edited to correct misspellings and grammatical errors, and add several editor's notes. The preservation of the essence of Dr. Russell's thoughts and teachings has been foremost in our minds.

Scientific investigation of Walter Russell's ideas gives the reward of deeper understanding into the nature of the Universe, and will serve as an inspiration and light into the next centuries. Technological application of his principles holds the promise of a non-polluting sustainable energy future that is presently so desperately needed.

It is with great hope and expectation for humanity's greater comprehension and use of *The Secret Of Light* that we offer this updated edition.

THE WAVE

IN THE WAVE LIES THE SECRET OF CREATION

AUTHOR'S FOREWORD

Jesus said, "GOD IS LIGHT," and no man of that day knew what He meant. The day is now here when all men must know what Jesus meant when He said "GOD IS LIGHT."

For within the secret of Light is vast knowledge yet unrevealed to man. Light is all there is; it is all we have to deal with, but we do not yet know what it is. The purpose of this message is to *tell* what it is.

Today's civilization has advanced far in knowing HOW to deal with matter but we do not know WHAT matter is nor the WHY of it. Nor do we know what energy, electricity, magnetism, gravitation and radiation are. Nor do we know the purpose of the inert gases and WHAT they are. Nor do we know the structure of the elemental atoms nor the gyroscopic principle which determines that structure. Nor are we aware of the fact that this is a two-way continuous universe of balance in all effects of motion and not a one-way discontinuous universe. Nor have we even yet heard of or suspected the most important of all principles in physics, THE VOIDANCE PRINCIPLE and the mirrors and lenses of space which are the cause of illusion in all moving things.

Nor do we even consider the entire material electric universe to be the illusion which it is; there being no reality to it whatsoever.

Nor have we the slightest inkling of the cause of curvature of space, nor the voidance of that curvature in planes of zero curvature at wave field boundaries. No one now knows how it is that crystals get their various shapes. It will amaze the world to know that those shapes of crystals are determined in space by the shapes of the wave fields which bound the various elemental structures.

Nor have we the slightest conception of what constitutes the life principle, nor the principle of growth, nor the simultaneous unfoldment-refoldment principle which repeats all patterns in Nature sequentially and records and voids them as they are repeated. Nor are we aware of that recording principle by means of which the Creator carries forth the sum totals of every sequential cycle in His unfolding and refolding universe unto the very end of its manifestations upon one planet and its beginning on a new one.

Nor are we dynamically aware of the souls and seeds of things. These roots of universal repetition are now but metaphysical abstractions to religion and physical guesswork to science.

Within the secret of Light is the answer to all of these heretofore unanswered questions, and many more, which the ages have not yet solved. This revelation of the nature of Light will be the inheritance of man in this coming New Age of greater comprehension. Its unfoldment will prove the existence of God by methods and standards acceptable to science and religion alike. It will lay a spiritual foundation under the present material one of science.

The two greatest elements in civilization, religion and science, will thus find unity in marriage of the two. Likewise human relationships will become more balanced because of greater knowledge of universal law which lies behind all of the processes which light uses to interweave the patterned forms of this electric wave universe.

There is no department of life which will not be vitally affected by this new knowledge of the nature of Light, from the university to the laboratory, from government to industry, and from nation to nation.

I therefore give it to you with all of its clarity as I myself have become aware of it from behind the scenes of this cosmic cinema of light illusion which is our universe.

WALTER RUSSELL

Other Books by Walter Russell

The Message of The Divine Iliad—Vol. I
The Message of The Divine Iliad—Vol. II
A New Concept of the Universe
The Self Multiplication Principle
The Secret of Working Knowingly With God
The Electric Nature of the Universe
The Sculptor Searches for Mark Twain's Immortality
The Fifth Kingdom Man
The Dawn of a New Day in Human Relations
The Immortality of Man
The Book of Early Whisperings
Your Day and Night

Walter Russell Co-author with Lao Russell

Home Study Course in Universal Law, Natural Science and Living Philosophy
Scientific Answer to Human Relations
Atomic Suicide?
The World Crisis—Its Explanation and Solution
A Vision Fulfilled!
The One-World Purpose—A Plan to Dissolve War by a Power More Mighty Than War

Books by Lao Russell

God Will Work With You But Not For You
Love—A Scientific & Living Philosophy of Love and Sex
Why You Cannot Die!—Reincarnation Explained

For catalog on additional books and teachings by Walter and Lao Russell, please write or phone:

The University of Science and Philosophy
Swannanoa, P.O. Box 520, Waynesboro Virginia 22980
(703) 942-5161
(800) 882-LOVE (5683) Book Orders

PART I

OMNISCIENCE

THE UNIVERSE OF KNOWING

PART II

OMNIPOTENCE

THE UNIVERSE OF POWER

PART III

OMNIPRESENCE

THE UNIVERSE OF BEING

POSTULATES AND DIAGRAMS

"I am the Light; I alone AM.

"What I am thou art. Thou art the Light. Thou art One with Me.

"Man may know me by desiring to know Me.

"To know Me is to be Me. Through My Light alone can man know Me.

"Man is Light when he knoweth that he is Light.

"Man is Me when he knoweth that he is Me.

"All men will come to Me in due time, but theirs is the agony of awaiting."

—*From* THE DIVINE ILIAD

THE SECRET OF LIGHT

Part I

OMNISCIENCE

The Universe of Knowing

Chapter I

THE ETERNAL QUESTION

"Who am I?"

"What am I?"

"Why am I?"

"Whither am I bound?"

"What is my relation to the universe, to man, and to God?"

"What is Truth? How am I to know Truth?"

"Whence cometh my power? What is the Source of my power?"

"How am I to find Balance? In my dealings with my fellow men, how am I to know that balance in our interchange which will enrich both him and me?"

"Countless are the religious teachings, and many are the commandments to goodness, but goodness is still veiled from my eyes like a thick mist which hides Thy Light which I vainly seek."

"I stumble in its darkness. Unbalanced I fall."

"O thou unseen One, tear from my eyes the blinding veil which hides the path to Thy Light, that I may find my way to Thee."

That is the cry of the ages.

That is the unanswered question which is arising from the heart of this awakening generation.

Civilization progresses in cycles. New comprehension periodically transforms mankind into higher beings. A new cycle of three thousand years duration is now in its birth throes.

God's omniscience, omnipotence and omnipresence are centered in the consciousness of every man; but few there are who know of the Oneness of their Self-Soul with the Universal Self-Soul. Man requires many millennia to begin to be aware of that. Each cycle of man brings him nearer to his awareness of his Oneness with the Light of his Self-Source.

Man lives in a bewildering complex world of EFFECT of which he knows not the CAUSE. Because of its seemingly infinite multiplicity and complexity, he fails to vision the simple underlying principle of Balance in all things. He, therefore, complexes Truth until its many angles, sides and facets have lost balance with each other and with him.

Truth is simple. Balance is simple. Rhythmic balanced interchange between all pairs of opposite expressions in Natural phenomena, and in human relations, is the consummate art of God's universe of Light. It is also the Law. In this one fundamental Universal Law lies the balanced continuity of all creative expression in God's electric wave universe of two conditioned lights in seeming motion which record God's One Whole Idea of Creation into countless seemingly separate parts of that Whole Idea.

THE VOICE WITHIN

The great unanswered question of man has a simple answer. The Silent Voice within every man is ceaselessly whispering it to his awakening consciousness. Every desire written upon the heart of man is carried to the Source, and its answer will come, but few there are who ask comprehensively and fewer still who hear.

Many are the ages of preparation for worthiness to hear it, for man's consciousness is insulated from his Source by the sensations of his electrically conditioned body which he wrongly thinks of as being his Mind and his personal Self.

What he calls his objective human mind is but the seat of electric sensations of his body. What he mistakes for thinking is but an electric awareness of things sensed and recorded within the cells of his brain for repetitive usage through what is termed "memories." Memories have no more relation to knowledge of Universal Mind which is in man than Victrola records are related to the source of their recordings.

What he thinks of as his living body is but an electrically motivated machine which simulates life through motion extended to it from its centering Self-Soul which alone lives and wills the body to move.

What he calls his subjective mind is his consciousness, his spiritual storehouse of all-knowledge, all-power, and all-presence. That consciousness is his Self, his ETERNAL Self through which his omniscience, omnipresence and omnipotence are expressed as he slowly becomes aware of their presence within him.

The electrically oscillating nerve-wires which operate his bodily mechanism act almost entirely through automatic reflexes and instinctive control, and to a very little extent through mental decisions. Each cell and organ of his body has an electrical awareness of its purpose and each fulfills that purpose without any mental action whatsoever upon the part of the Intelligence which occupies that body. The heartbeat, for example, is purely automatic. The white corpuscles of the blood rush to repair an injury to the body as automatically as a bell rings when a button is pushed.

In this body and its electric recording brain, man thinks that he thinks and lives, loves and dies. He thinks himself conscious while awake and unconscious when sleeping; unaware that in all Nature there is no such condition as unconsciousness when sensation ceases in sleep.

Man does not say that his tooth is unconscious when it is put to sleep by short-circuiting the electric current in the nerve-wire which gives sensed electrical awareness to his tooth. He knows that his tooth cannot be conscious, but he does not know that his body cannot be conscious.

Nor does he yet know that consciousness never sleeps, never changes, for consciousness in man is his immortality. It is the Light which he is unknowingly seeking but assumes that the sensation of his brain is his thinking.

Man is still new. He is barely out of the dark of his jungle. For the million or more years of his unfolding he has relied upon sensation for his actions and the evidence of his senses for his knowing. He has been aware of the spirit in him only a very few thousands of years. In this beginning of his new awareness he is confused, knowing not which is Mind in him, which is consciousness in him and which is sensation.

He has not yet learned that bodies are but Self-created mechanisms which manifest their centering Self, and that Self manifests God as One with it. Likewise he has not yet learned that bodies neither live nor die, but repeat themselves continuously and forever as all idea of Mind likewise repeats itself.

The wheel, for example, is a mechanism consisting of a hub, spokes and a rim. A little part of the wheel touches the ground, feels it, then leaves it, to disappear from reach of the sensations which connect rim, spokes and ground.

But then it reappears.

When that happens to man we say, "He was born, lived and died." When it happens to the apple, the flame, or the tree, we say, "The apple was eaten, the flame has gone out and the tree has decayed." We say that because only a small part of the cycle of any idea comes within the range of our senses. The larger part of the cycle is beyond our range of perception, just as the larger part of the wheel is beyond the sensed perception of the ground.

We do not yet know that the invisible part of the cycles of all idea is as continuous as the wheel is continuous. The cycle of the apple is light reaching from the sun and earth to that positive half of the apple cycle which we hold in our hand. The negative half of the cycle is light returning to sun and earth for repetition as another manifestation of the eternal idea of the apple. The same is true of the flame, the tree or any other part of the One Whole Idea of Creation.

The flame "goes out" to our sensing. But it still IS. Likewise the tree, the forest, mountain, planet and nebula of the far heavens appear, disappear and as surely reappear.

Likewise man appears to disappear and reappear again and again in countless cycles to express eternal life of the spirit in eternal repetitions of that part of the man cycle which the body of man can sense.

Man never dies. He is as continuous as eternity is continuous. Jesus rightly said that man shall not see death, for there is no death to see or to know.

Likewise the body of man does not live, and having never lived it cannot die. The spirit alone lives. The body but manifests the spirit. That which we think of as life in the spirit of man manifests itself by willing the body to act. Actions thus made by the body under the command of its centering Soul have no motivative power or intelligence in themselves; they are but machines motivated by an omniscient and omnipotent intelligence extended to them.

These things we do not yet know, for man is in his infancy. He is but beginning to know the Light.

BE YE FOREVER TRANSFORMED

Man is forever seeking the Light to guide him on that long tortuous road which leads from his body's jungle to the mountain top of his awakening soul.

Man is forever finding that Light, and is being forever transformed as he finds it.

And as he finds it he gradually finds the Self of him which IS the Light.

And as he becomes more and more transformed by the God-Light of the awakening Self within him, he leaves the jungle farther below him in the dark.

There are those who seek the Light who are discouraged because they seemingly cannot find it, wholly unaware that they have forever been finding it. Unknowing ones expect to find it all at once in some blinding flash of all-power, all-knowledge and all-presence.

It does not come that way until one is nearing his mountain top. Man cannot bear much of the Light at a time while his body is still new and too near its jungle. All who are well out of the jungle have already found enough of the Light to illume their way out of its dark depths.

He who is far out of the jungle and still seeks the Light in the High-heavens is forever finding it, and is forever being transformed as he finds it.

One cannot for one moment remove his seeking eyes from his High-heaven, for ever so slight a glimpse below into the dark brings him back to the fears of the dark, which tempt him to plunge back into them.

Look ye, therefore, forever upward into the High-heavens of inspiration, where glory awaits the fearless, all-knowing seekers of Beauty in the purity of the universal Light.

To him whose eyes are in the High-heavens, the Light will forever come, and he will be forever transformed as he finds it.

The dark road from his jungle to his mountain top of glory becomes ever more illumined during the ascent from body to spirit.

It is a hard, but glorious road to climb. All must make the climb.

THE ASCENT OF MAN FROM THE DARK TO THE LIGHT is the forever repetitive play of man on the planets of suns.

When all mankind has found the Light, the play will be finished. Likewise this planet will be finished as an abode for man. It will then be rolled off into its ever expanding orbit while Venus is gradually being rolled into place to become the stage for the next repetition of THE ASCENT OF MAN in this solar system.

We actors of the play must, therefore, be content with the lines of the play revealed to each of us in Light. We must, likewise, be ever joyous at our continuous transformation, as each one of us learns our part, line by line, the better to fulfill it worthily.

All parts of the play are experiences which become the action of the play. All man's experiences are part of his unfolding. Each experience is a part of his journey from the dark to the Light. All experiences are steps in that journey to his mountain top of glory. All experiences, therefore, are good experiences.

There is naught but GOOD. There is no evil.

There is naught but LIFE. There is no death.

"I am the One Whole, the ALL.

"Glorify thou Me, the One Whom I am, for I am ALL, and no other is.

"I, the sexless One, am Unity.

"What I am thou art, for thou art Me; thou art the Whole.

"Glorify thou thy Self, for in so doing thou art glorifying Me.

"I, the One Whole, am knowing Mind. I exist to think. All thinking is Light of My knowing but My thinking is not Me.

"I am Creator, creating with My thinking.

"Out of My Light of knowing are My two lights of thinking born as sexed pairs of opposites for repetition as sexed pairs of opposites.

"To think is to create. I create with Light. Nothing is which is not Light.

"I think idea. Light registereth My idea in the two sexed lights of My thinking, and form is born in the image of My thinking.

"Form hath no existence, nor have My imaginings. These exist not, for they are not Me. I alone existeth; I, the ALL.

"I create my imaged body with the in-breathing of My pulsing universe of Me.

"My universe is My image; but My image is not Me.

"All things are My image, but they are not Me, e'en though I am in them and they in Me."

—*From* THE DIVINE ILIAD

Chapter II

CREATOR AND CREATION

God, the Creator, is all there IS; all that EXISTS.

God's creating universe of matter in motion appears to exist. To our senses it sequentially disappears, to reappear. It has no reality. It but simulates reality through the illusion of two-way projected lights in motion.

God, the Creator, is the One Being, the One Person, the One Mind, the One Thinker, the One Self, the One Life, the One Soul, the One Power, the One Reality.

God's Creation is the imaged patterned form of God's imagining, built in His image. It is the body of God, the record of His thinking, created by Him for expressing the One-ness of Life, Love, Mind, Soul and Power which is in Him alone.

THE ONE LIGHT

God is Light. God is Universal Mind. Mind is Light. Mind knows.

Mind thinks what it knows. Mind thinks in two opposed lights simultaneously projected from their centering white Light Source and sequentially repeated in cycles.

God's thinking and imagining are qualities of God's knowing. God's knowing Mind is timeless and still. So also are God's thinking and imagining timeless and still. So, likewise, man's thinking and imagining are as timeless and still as is his knowing.

Stillness never can be motion, or become motion, but it can appear to be. Motion merely seems, but stillness always is. The universal equilibrium can never be other than its own balance but it can seem to be. The illusion which is motion springs from stillness and returns to stillness. This is a universe of rest. There is naught but rest in the universe.

Mind knows its One Idea of Creation as One Whole.

Mind thinks its One Whole idea into seeming parts. Hence the illusion of motion which we call Creation, and the illusion of substance which we call matter.

Matter, motion, time, change, dimension and substance have no existence. The Light of knowing Mind alone exists.

There is but One Mind and One Thinker.

The One Light of knowing Mind is Self of God. It is the Universal Self which centers all omnipresent self-creating bodies of God-Selves. This self creating universe is the Mind imagined body of God, and record of God's thinking.

We can KNOW God. We cannot KNOW His body but we can SEE it. Likewise we can KNOW man. We cannot KNOW the body of man but we can SEE it. What God is man is. God and man are ONE.

OUR SEEMING DUALITY

We seemingly live in two universes; the still cosmic Mind universe of KNOWING and the moving thought-of-Mind rhythmic wave universe of SENSING.

We cannot *sense* the cosmic universe of God's knowing nor can we *know* the thought-wave universe of God's thinking.

The cosmic Mind universe of the One Light of all-knowing is all that is.

The vibrating thought-wave universe of sensing merely seems.

THE COSMIC GOD LIGHT

The one still Light of God is the cosmic Light which watches over all creating things at countless points locatable by man, but invisible to man.

Man's senses have misled him into believing in a force called magnetism which attracts compass needles and lifts tons of steel. These phenomena of motion are due to electricity and not to magnetism. The cosmic Light is absolutely still. It neither attracts nor repels.

We now need to comprehend the nature and purpose of the "magnetic poles" of suns, planets and all other moving extensions of the One Light. Likewise, we need to know the nature and purpose of the two electric workers which interweave this light mirage of seeming motion and dissolve it sequentially for rebuilding. This will give a foundation of knowledge to man which will enable him to see behind the illusions which deceive his senses.

The time has come in the history of man's journey from his material jungle to his spiritual mountain top when it is imperative that he must live more and more in the cosmic Light universe of knowing, and less in the electric wave universe of sensing.

Man must know that his power lies in the stillness of his centering Self and not in the motion by means of which he manifests that stillness. He must know that his Self is God in him. Also he must know gradually the dawning awareness of the cosmic Light of God in him, for with it comes an awareness of his purposefulness in manifesting the Light and the power to manifest it.

Man must now know the universe of God for what it is instead of what his senses have made him believe it to be.

Also, he must know that this forever creating universe which seems so real to him is but a cosmic cinema, conceived by the Master Playwright. It is but an electrically projected, spectrum-colored light and sound-wave motion picture play of CAUSE AND EFFECT thrown on the black screen of imaged space and time.

The CAUSE is real. The EFFECT is but a simulation of the reality.

The Self of man is cause. His self-creating body is effect.

God's universe of magnetic Light is static.

God's perpetually creating electric wave universe of two moving lights is dynamic. It forever moves. The two moving lights are projected through each other from the static One to create the illusion of the idea they but manifest. The illusion which manifests the idea of Creation through seeming motion is not the idea which it seemingly manifests.

Creation is the product of Mind-knowing expressed in form by Mind-Thinking.

The product of Mind is not the idea which it simulates. No idea of Mind is ever created. It is but simulated by form and motion. Idea is eternal and belongs to God's still universe of knowing.

Form of idea in matter is transient but is eternally repeated as transient form of idea.

THE POSITIVE PRINCIPLE

The foundation of the spiritual universe is stillness; the balanced stillness of the One magnetic Light of God.

Balanced stillness is the *Positive Principle* of stability and unity. In it there are no negations.

THE NEGATIVE PRINCIPLE

The foundation of the physical universe is motion; the ever-changing motion arising out of pairs of unbalanced conditions which must forever move to seek the balanced stillness of unity from which they sprang as multiple pairs of units.

Unbalanced motion is the Negative Principle of instability, multiplicity and separateness which is this physical universe of electric octave waves of opposed lights.

In the Negative Principle there is no positive. It is composed entirely of pairs of negations which are forever voiding each other, cancelling each other's action and reaction, thus negating each other by never allowing either one to exceed its fixed zero of universal stillness.

QUALITY BEGETS QUANTITIES

The still magnetic Light universe of God's knowing is an invisible, unchanging, unconditioned and unmeasurable quality from which visible, changing, conditioned and measurable quantities spring to simulate those qualities through two-way wave motion.

There is no one word in any language to express that quality so we must use many words, all having the same meaning but different connotations.

These words are mind, consciousness, love, life, truth, desire, knowledge, power, balance and law.

The God-quality of the One Light is seemingly transformed into quantities by being divided into pairs of oppositely-conditioned light pressures of this electric universe. These divided pairs are then multiplied into countless octave wave units of light pressures and set in opposite directioned motion to create the illusion of sequence, change, dimension, condition and time in a universe where none of these effects of motion exist.

The calm sea, for example, is an unchanging, unmeasurable quality of oneness, of sameness and stillness. Upon its calm surface there is no change, nothing to count or to measure.

The moment that quantities of waves spring from that quality of calm, those quantities can be measured. Likewise, they are forever changing. Nor are there two points in them which are similarly conditioned.

This creating electric universe is composed of moving light waves which sprang from a calm sea of the One still Light.

It is a universe of moving pairs of quantities which simulate the quality of stillness from which those quantities spring. The quantities of divided and conditioned pairs of opposite lights which thus simulate the One are not the One they simulate.

The Creator is One Mind indivisible. Creation is One Whole Idea of Mind divided into countless simulated ideas of mind, through motion. The simulation of Idea thus expressed is not the idea that it expresses.

Parts of the One Whole Idea are only seeming. There are no two separate or separable things in the universe. There is but One Whole Simulation of the One Whole Idea.

"Everything that is is of everything else that is.
All things are indissolubly united."

—*From* THE DIVINE ILIAD

Every happening anywhere happens everywhere. The milkweed fluff floating lazily in the summer sky affects the balance of the whole universe of suns and galaxies. Every part of the universe moves in interdependent unison as the wheels of a watch move in unison. The watch wheels are geared together mechanically. The rhythmic wave universe is geared together electrically.

The entire universe is one and must be kept in balance as one. Changes of condition in any one part are simultaneously reflected in every other part, and are sequentially repeated in it.

"Say thou these things in words of man's knowing, for, verily I say, I am within all things, without all things, and involved in all things, for I am everywhere.

"All things are omnipresent, for all things extend from Mind of Me, and I am omnipresent.

"All omnipresent things are omniscient, for I am within them, and I am omniscient. When man's consciousness telleth him of My presence within and without him he will then know all things, for I know all things, and I am he.

"All thinking things manifesteth all power when consciousness within them recognizeth their omnipotence. Until then, things are naught but things, manifesting me not, being but blank slates upon which to write My mighty thoughts for blind eyes.

"For I am omnipotent. I give all power to him who asketh but no one may ask of Me who is not aware of Me. See thou to it that man well knoweth that, and manifest thou thyself that principle of power in thine own works.

"For I say to all the imaged forms of My imagining, that power lieth in them to manifest the balanced Light which centereth them, by making the One Light appear as two unbalanced lights which interchange sequentially but equally.

"And again I say that all things which man senseth are but waves of dual light which record My electric thinking in the imagined forms of My imagining.

"And also I say that the imagined forms of My imagining have no Being, for I alone have Being."

—*From* THE DIVINE ILIAD

Chapter III

SENSATION AND CONSCIOUSNESS

God is consciousness. Consciousness is static. Consciousness is the KNOWING of mind. Knowing is static.

Consciousness is the spiritual awareness of Being, of all-knowing, all-power and all-presence.

Thinking is electric.

God's thinking is expressed by two-way moving wave extensions from consciousness, like a lever swinging upon a fixed fulcrum, or like waves extending from the calm sea. Thought expression is dynamic. Thinking belongs to the electrically sensed and conditioned vibrating universe of motion. Thinking is the motionless principle in light which creates the illusion of motion.

The Self of man belongs to the static, invisible, conscious, unconditioned universe of KNOWING. We express knowing in the dynamic, visible, electrically conditioned universe of sensation.

Sensation is the electrical awareness of motion simulating the spiritual QUALITIES of the One Idea by creating imaged QUANTITIES of separate forms which seem to have substance.

Consciousness is real. Sensation simulates reality through motion of interchanging lights, but the mirage of a city is not the city it reflects.

Confusion and misunderstanding as to whether we are thinking consciously from knowledge or sensing electrically from memory records stored in our brains have led us to the necessity of distinguishing between the two by the common usage of such terms as "the human mind" and "mortal mind." We know full well, while using them, that there is but the One Mind of the One Living God of Love.

The universal Mind centers every particle and mass in this universe: animal, vegetable or mineral, electron, atom or sun.

Man is the only unit in Creation who has *conscious awareness* of the Spirit within him and *electrical awareness* of dually conditioned light acting upon his senses. All other units of Creation have electrical awareness only.

Man alone can be freed from body to think with God, to talk with God and be inspired by His centering Light. All other units of Creation are limited in their actions to automatic reflexes from sensed memories built up through ages of sensing and recording such sensing as instinct.

Likewise the same confusion leads us to the adoption of such terms as "subconscious mind," and "superconscious mind."

There is but One Mind functioning universally within all creating things, and that One Mind is not stratified nor divided into the more or less. There are no differing conditions of the One Mind, nor are there different kinds of minds.

IMAGINATION

God is the imaginer of His One Idea.

All imagining is God's imagining.

All creating forms in this thought universe of God's imagining are built in the image of His imagining, creating "in His image."

All forms in this creating universe of imagined forms are but electric recordings of God's imaginings. They have no existence. Records of Idea are not the idea they record.

They have no substance. They are but black and white lights of sun-centered wave fields of space assembled in vibrating systems to simulate substance in an objective universe which is not, but *seems* to be.

God's imagining never began and will never end.

It was not "created" at some remote past time by some vast cosmic event, as commonly believed. Nor is it condemned to a "heat-death" by expansion into nothingness.

This is a creating universe, not a created one.

God did not begin to imagine at some fixed time, for time does not exist. This light-wave universe which records God's knowing by His thinking and imagining is as eternal as God's thinking is eternal.

INSPIRATION

Inspiration is the language of Light which man uses to talk with God.

Inspiration is that deep awareness of the consciousness of Being which differentiates the genius or mystic from the being of average intelligence.

Inspiration in man is accompanied by an intense mental ecstasy which is characteristic of all who become intensely conscious of their closeness to God.

Inspired geniuses forget their bodies while deeply conscious of their existence as wholly Mind. Their bodies, thus forgotten, act almost automatically in obedience to instinct and cell memory reflexes.

Inspired geniuses translate God's knowing into words of man for the soul of man. They uplift all mankind by reinspiring all who listen to their ecstatic words and rhythms.

He who attunes his heart to the messages of genius purifies himself. No impurity can there be in his heart for verily he then is in communion with the Holy One.

"Man alone of all My creating things hath begun to hear My whisperings. Since his beginning My still small Voice hath whispered within him that I am he and he Me; but even now barbaric man on thy small new world heareth dully, and maketh idols which he treasures before Me, for he is still new. He is still but in the ferment of his early brewing.

"For I say, that all things which floweth from Life of Me have Life of Me flowing through them, e'en to the least of these; but, I say, that e'en though My Light of immortal Life floweth through those mortal symbols of My thinking, It toucheth them not in Its passing.

"When they shall know the Light of Me in them, then they shall be Me and I them."

—*From* THE DIVINE ILIAD

Chapter IV

COSMIC CONSCIOUSNESS

Beyond the genius is the mystic.

The mystic is one who has attained cosmic consciousness by a complete severance of the seats of consciousness and sensation. He is then almost totally unaware of his body and is totally aware of the Light of God centering him. Omniscience comes to him in that timeless blinding flash of light which is characteristic of a complete severance. This experience was described in the illumination of St. Paul. Every timeless flash of intense inspiration which comes to any man is a partial illumination, for inspiration is the manner in which new knowledge comes to man from the cosmos.

Of all mystics, Jesus was the outstanding example of all time. He was the only One in all history to have known complete cosmic-conscious unity with God.

The Bible refers to cosmic-conscious experience as "the illumination" or "being in the Light" or "in the Spirit."

In all history less than forty cases of partial cosmic consciousness are known, and probably not more than three of these anywhere nearly approached the complete state of illumination experienced by the Nazarene.

Cosmic consciousness is the ultimate goal of all mankind. All will know it before the long journey of man is finished, but there are many in this new age just dawning who are ready for it in part, if not fully.

Many desire it fully, but it is best that it come bit by bit for the complete severance is very dangerous. The ecstasy of this supreme experience is so great that one does not wish to come back. The power of severance of soul from body is within easy accomplishment, but to step back into the body is very difficult.

The way to gradually attain cosmic consciousness is to intensify one's conscious awareness by much aloneness and companionship with God while manifesting Him in every moment and in every task of life.

Moment-by-moment companionship with God brings with it so great a realization of Oneness with Him that the transformation into that full realization of unity is apt to take place at any time.

The deterrent to cosmic consciousness is the feeling that God is far away instead of being within, and that we can reach that far away God only through sources outside of ourselves.

"He who would interpret the rhythm of Me in art must walk his path in ecstasy, undiverted by deviations, that he may see Me only and hear naught but Me.

"Say thou to man these words:

"I am the source of inspiration. To him who seeketh inspiration through Me, I say: Learn thou to walk my path strongly in the Light, for in the dark thou canst not find thy way to Me. The path to Me is Light, and by it thou canst well see thy way to Me.

"I am the soul of art. To him whose soul would touch My Soul, and feel the heartbeat of its mighty rhythm, I say: In so far as thou knowest thyself as Light, shalt thou know Me as Light.

"I am Beauty. In Beauty must man be born anew. Through Beauty must knowing man become ecstatic Man.

"To him who would add ecstasy to his knowing I say: Seek Me in Truth; for only in the rhythm of Truth shalt thou find ecstasy.

"Verily I say, the creations of Ecstatic Man are My creations, for they are balanced things, and I am balance.

"To him who wouldeth create unbalance I say: Un-truth exists not in My house. I alone hold balance; and the eyes of those who see through Me are immune from all but balance.

"For I am Balance. And I am Energy, and I am Rest. I am the Light of Love and Truth. Upon that foundation have I laid the corner-stone of My universe."

—*From* THE DIVINE ILIAD

Chapter V

CREATIVE EXPRESSION

Inspired man alone can create enduring things. To create we must first conceive.

To conceive we must stop thinking and KNOW. All sensing must cease. There is no power in thinking. Thinking but expresses the power which lies in knowing. We must project our Selves into the still Light of knowing to commune with God. We must become one with God to conceive idea in order to produce the form of that idea. A concept must precede its manifestation in form.

The culture of the entire race is given to it by the few inspired ones who know God in them. They alone know immortality.

The art of a civilization long outlives the civilization. The pyramids of Egypt still speak of the creation of a race which is long gone from the face of the earth. The sculptural and architectural beauty of Greece still tell us of a type of creative genius which has never been excelled. The great in the arts are few. "Art alone endures. All else passes."

Great art can be created only by working moment by

moment with God as co-creator. When man and God thus work together they commune one with the other as One Person. The language of their communion is the language of Light which man calls "inspiration."

When man works alone, his works are as the winds which blow. When man works with God as co-creator, his works are forever enduring.

Every great genius manifests this law: that he is One with the God-Mind, that God in him is the source of every thought and that he is inspired by that omniscience and omnipotence within him which make his work enduring.

"All knowledge existeth. All knowledge cometh to man in its season. Cosmic messengers periodically give to man such knowledge of My cosmos as man is able to comprehend, but that which he can bear is like unto a thimbleful out of the mighty ocean, for man is but beginning to comprehend.

"When man knoweth Light then he will know no limitations, but man must know the Light for himself and none there can be who can make words of it, for Light knoweth Light and there need be no words."

—*From* THE DIVINE ILIAD

Chapter VI

KNOWLEDGE

Knowledge is cosmic. It belongs to the still Light of the positive principle. It never can become a property of the two negations which constitute this mirage universe of matter in motion.

To "know all things" means to have all knowledge of the Whole One Idea of the cosmos as CAUSE. It does not mean knowledge of created things which are effect of cause. The whole Cosmic Idea is simple. It can be known by anyone of average intelligence. Its bewildering complexities lie in effect of cause.

Man cannot *know* transient effect. He can KNOW cause only. He can but comprehend effect. Man cannot know a sunset sky, for example, but he can comprehend it if he knows its cause. Knowledge is, therefore, limited to cause.

All knowledge exists. All mankind can have it for the asking. It is within man, awaiting his awareness of its all-presence.

Knowledge cannot be acquired by the brain from without; it must be "recollected" from within the consciousness of Self. Gradually dawning conscious awareness is but gradual recollection of the all-knowing which has always been within man.

Man cannot acquire knowledge from books or schools. He can but acquire information that way, but information is not knowledge until it is recognized by the spiritual consciousness of man, just as food is not nourishment for the body until it becomes a part of the blood stream. Information gained by motion of the senses must be returned to the stillness of the Source before it becomes knowledge.

For the same reason man cannot acquire knowledge from the so-called "facts of matter," for there are no facts of matter in a universe of transient matter in motion. All matter in motion is but a series of illusions which deceive man into drawing wrong conclusions.

It is impossible for man to draw right conclusions from his observation of matter in motion until he has acquired the ability to translate dynamic effect back to cause. This he can do only through decentration to the One Light of his conscious awareness of the Source of all knowledge. Until he knows the WHY of effect and its deceptions, he has no knowledge whatsoever upon which he can rely. He has naught but unreliable information.

Information concerning the body, for example, does not give knowledge concerning cause of body, or of the body's relationship to the universe. Information of birth and death of the body, on the assumption that the body is Self, never can lead to knowledge that body is not Self, or that Self is immortal.

Nor can information concerning the material body alone, its chemistry and its functionings, heal the body. Bodies manifest life, but life is cosmic. Life is not in the body. Life is spirit, and spirit is still. Life is not chemistry or germ of matter. To heal the body so that it can manifest life of the spirit Self of the body, one must give the unbalanced body the balance of the spirit. Knowledge of the Light can alone do this. All the information in the world will not heal a body unassisted by the Light in him who heals and in him who is being healed.

"I am LIGHT, but the Light which is Me is not the sensed light of the sensed universe of My creation.

"I, the Creator, think. I think in two lights extended from the One Light of Me, yet those two lights are not Me, nor is My thinking Me.

"Verily I say, I give of Me and I take away; for I am the Imaginer who builds image forms to tear apart to build anew.

"I am thinking Mind, forever thinking the changing image of My unchanging self.

"My image changes ever with the changing of the two lights of My thinking, though I, My Self, change not.

"All things change, and their changing still images Me, yet they are not Me."

—*From* THE DIVINE ILIAD

Chapter VII

KNOWLEDGE VERSUS THINKING

Man's knowledge is his power. His thinking is the expression of that power. The expression of power is not power; therefore thinking is not power.

As man gradually becomes aware of his omniscience, his thinking intensifies in voltage in proportion to the increase in awareness of his omniscience.

Thinking is an electric wave extension from the centering fulcrum of knowledge which seemingly divides knowledge into ideas and sets those ideas in motion to create forms of ideas as product of knowledge.

Man's knowledge is like a deep well of still water. His thinking is like a two-way pump which divides the QUALITY of that stillness into QUANTITIES of parts and sets them flowing.

That is what the objective universe is, quantities of many seemingly separate forms of idea, all of which are but parts of the One Whole Idea.

Each seemingly separate part is a dynamic extension of the One Static Unity, but separateness only *seems*, for all are indissolubly bound together in light as one part.

Knowledge is the foundation of man's concepts.

Thinking transfers concepts into product. The quality

of man's product depends upon the degree of awareness of his knowledge and not upon the quality, quantity or intensity of his thinking.

Water cannot be drawn from an empty well, nor can clear water be drawn from a muddied well. Likewise good product cannot come from intensive thinking unless knowledge backs that thinking.

No idea of Mind can ever become matter. Idea of product can never become product. Moreover, no expression of anything in Nature is the idea which it expresses.

The product of idea is not the idea it simulates. Idea is cosmic and cannot be produced in matter. Idea must be conceived in the Mind before it can be simulated as product. Conceptions belong solely to the magnetic God-Light and never become matter.

A lever, for example, moving upon its fulcrum, expresses the idea of power by motion, but the idea of power is in the still fulcrum source of power. It is not in the moving lever. The lever would be both powerless and motionless if it did not have the stillness of the fulcrum from which to extend the simulation of power.

A watch expresses the idea of time, but the watch is not time. Likewise it expresses the idea of mechanical principles, but the watch is not the idea which is expressed by those mechanical principles.

The printed poem is not the idea expressed in the

poem. That printed poem has no meaning to anyone whose intelligence is insufficient to reflect the idea from the composer's mind to his own. No idea of mind ever becomes matter.

Likewise neither the musical composition on the printed page, nor the art of music which issues as sounds from musical instruments is the inspired idea of the musician. Inspiration can never be produced. It can but be reflected from one inspired mind to another recognizing one. Idea and inspiration may be echoed from spirit to spirit but they can never become product of matter in motion.

"Man's sense-seeing with his eyes binds him to the illusion of My dual thinking, for I but build illusion with My dual thinking for his sense-seeing.

"Sense-seeing binds man to forms and things, while Mind-knowing opens doors of glory to the opposed threads of Light with which I weave all idea of Mind into forms of many moving things.

"Mind-seeing decentrates unto the farthest reaches of My universe of Me, and sees all forms as One.

"With his seeing eyes man sees Light as matter energized, but senses not that the energy of matter is the Light of My divided thinking. With man's unseeing eyes of spirit he knows the Light of Me, the Source, and knows that he is bound in Me as One, and I in him.

"Behold in Me thy God of Love, the One, inseparable."

—*From* THE DIVINE ILIAD

Chapter VIII

THINKING VERSUS SENSING

Man is still primate with very few exceptions. He has not yet learned to think powerfully from knowledge. He is just beginning to think as an extension of knowledge.

We sense electrically and mistake that electrical sensing of observed effects for thinking. Sensing is not thinking. Sensation is but an electrical awareness of wave motion by other waves.

We mistake the electrical records of the information which our brains have recorded as sensation, for thinking and for knowledge.

Information thus acquired by the senses is not knowledge, however. A man may have vast information and skill but have very little knowledge.

The greatest scientists of today, for example, are well informed. They know how to do wonderful things but do they know the WHY of what they do?

Information from observed effects, and skills in putting those effects together for useful purposes, have multiplied vastly since man first observed natural phenomena. His sense of observation told him how to make a boat; then a sail for the boat. He then discovered the wheel and fire. Electric awareness of effects of motion, plus memory, plus the power to reason objectively, gave him the ability to do this. Very little of it has been due to either thinking or knowledge.

We thus confuse sensing for thinking and knowing when, factually, we have been but functioning through sensed electrical awareness acquired from information.

The "information" thus conveyed is electrical, not mental. The telegraph message which goes over any wire is not the thought conveyed by that message. Even the typed telegram is not the thought conveyed by it. Its symbols inform the thinker of the thought conveyed by it, but it is not the thought.

Thus it is that our vast mechanistic, electrically motivated universe is inter-sensitized for the purpose of informing every nerve ganglion in every cell of every organic and inorganic part of it of the condition of every other part of it.

OUR SUPPOSEDLY FIVE SENSES

In speaking of an electrical awareness which we call sensation, we think of our senses as five in number. These are the senses of seeing, hearing, tasting, smelling and feeling.

All of these five senses are but the one sense of feeling. We do not have five senses. Seeing is a sensation of feeling light waves through our eyes. Hearing is a sensation of feeling light waves through our ears. Tasting and smelling are sensations of feeling light waves reacting upon mouth and nostrils.

All variation in sense of feeling is due to a difference of electric conditioning in pulsing wave matter. If pulsing wave matter is but an electric wave record of thought, sensation likewise is but an electric wave record of thought. Neither of them have reality. Neither of them are the thought they record.

It also follows that if matter, motion and substance are electric records of thought, then sensation has no reality—for sensation is but an electrical awareness of wave motion by other waves.

It likewise follows that if matter, motion and substance are electric wave recordings of thought, then electricity which records thought, and thought itself, are nonexistent.

There is but one thing in this universe—LIGHT— the still Light of all Knowing. The One Light which is God. God alone lives. His thinking and imagining is Knowing; the Knowing universe is all that is; Knowing Mind is still. There is no activity whatsoever in the universe of either spirit or matter.

EMPIRICAL KNOWLEDGE

Man's present civilization is erected upon the foundation of empirical knowledge obtained through his senses. What is empirical knowledge? The definition in the dictionary is: "conclusions founded upon experiment and observation alone."

In other words, the so-called "knowledge" upon which man relies is founded upon the evidence of his senses, or more simply, upon the nonexistent waves of motion of a nonexistent substance.

That fact is the answer as to why mankind has, as yet, practically no knowledge. During his amoeba and jungle days, he lived a purely sensed existence. His body cells were controlled entirely by instinctive flux threads of light extended to him directly from the Creator.

MAN IS STILL NEW

Out of millions of such years, he has had but a few thousand years since the dawn of consciousness awakened in him the slightest suspicion of his spiritual inheritance.

The advance of man since the first messengers of God appeared on earth to kindle an awakening spark in him, has been based upon information gained by his senses and stored in his electric brain as memory records of sensed observations. These observations he has reasoned into sensed conclusions by an electrically sensitized brain.

All of such conclusions which are based upon the evidence of senses have within them the elements of deception which characterize all effects of motion in this three dimensional universe of illusion.

Man is aware of some of these illusions, such as those of perspective. He is aware of the fact that railroad tracks do not meet upon the horizon, but he is not aware of the fact that all effects of motion are not what they seem to be. He is thus misled into forming conclusions which have no relation to Nature whatsoever. One can have no knowledge of effect, for all knowledge lies in cause. Our new fundamental laws and principles must be based upon knowledge of cause.

LAWS BASED UPON ILLUSION

Newton, for example, confessedly did not know what gravitation was, yet wrote laws concerning it based upon his observation as to what gravitation did to an apple. Also, he concluded that the moon would fall upon the earth if it were not for its motion. He even proved this mathematically, not being aware of the fact that those same mathematical formulae would apply to every satellite, planet and star in the heavens, as well as to every electron in every atom, none of which are falling into their primaries.[1]

Observers in natural phenomena are still calculating the age of the universe and weight of the earth. The universe is ageless. It had no beginning. Likewise the earth has no weight in respect to anything else in the universe. Every orb in the heavens is in perfect balance with every other orb.

MESSENGERS OF THE LIGHT

What little knowledge man has acquired during these last few thousand years has been given to him by the very few geniuses, prophets, mystics and other messengers of the Light who have come to reinspire mankind with their inspired knowledge.

From these rare few, the beginnings of our culture have sprung. Without them there would be no understanding of beauty in the world. Without beauty man would still be barbarian. Through beauty alone will he gradually become consciously aware of his oneness with the Light.

When man knows the Light he will know all things. Today that Light is so dim in all mankind that no one has as yet fathomed the secret of Light, or of gravitation, radiation, electricity, growth, life, reincarnation or the wave.

The day has now dawned when he will know these things. This is man's inheritance for this New Age.

"Behold in Me the One Light from which a seeming two lights appear as pairs of rhythmically interchanging opposites. These are My light messengers. They are My workers which build My imaged forms and give them back to Me devoid of form.

"They are the pulsing heartbeat of My body, the Makers of forever borning cycles of My imagining in forms of things.

"The two are equal halves of one. They never can become one. They forever interchange to simulate a balanced unity which they never find for they never can be aught but two.

"From Me one light extendeth to give form to My imaginings, and give them pulsebeat to simulate eternal Life in them which IS in Me. The other light dissolveth that form and giveth it back to Me unquickened for resurrection in My rest to repeat My imaginings.

"Say thou, therefore, that life is eternal in man through eternities of resurrections of him in Me. And say thou, also, that his resurrection is his own, for he is ONE with Me.

"Thus is My imagined dual light universe born, dissolved and reborn; concentrated, decentrated and reconcentrated; integrated, disintegrated and reintegrated forever and forever in My imagined universe of imagined time and space.

"And, behold, each of My pairs of opposite expressions of Me are reborn through Me as the other one. Again I say, there is naught but rebirth in Me. There is no death.

"Go thou and tell to man that both life and death are but mirrors of each other which becometh each other in their forever interpassing through each other to their still fulcrum in My knowing, from which both sprang into seeming being to record the imaged forms of My thinking."

—*From* THE DIVINE ILIAD

Chapter IX

SENSING BINDS ALL THINGS

The electric inter-sensitizing of the two pulsing light extensions of the One still Light is for the purpose of recording thought-patterns in matter.

Mind knows but one Idea as a whole. Thought is Idea taken apart and patterned as separate idea. Thought is patterned idea electrically expressed and electrically recorded in matter by its two pulsing, interchanging lights.

This universe of matter in motion is but the electric record of thought. The process of recording is to take the One undivided Universal Idea apart and express it as many seemingly divided parts. This gives form and multiplicity into many seeming parts and things of a universe of but one thing.

Electricity is the servant of the God-Mind. Electricity expresses the desire in the God-Mind for creative expression by seemingly dividing the One still light into transient waves of spectrum divided positive-negative colors of light.

This entire universe of seeming substantiality consists solely of transient light waves in seeming motion.

Motion itself is illusion.

SEEMING SEPARATENESS

All patterned thought creations of God or man are the interweavings of the spectrum colors of the two electric opposites of light-waves into the patterned designs of those thoughts.

Creation might be likened to the tapestry weaver who KNOWS the one idea as a whole, then THINKS it into parts, then RECORDS those parts by interweaving their spectrum colors into the many forms which, together, manifest the whole idea.

To exemplify our meaning, consider any one part of the whole idea of Creation—iron, for example. Iron is a separate part of the whole.

We think of iron as a hard, cold metal with certain properties which make it possible for us to manufacture it into many products. When iron is in its frozen condition, we do not think of it as light, but we can photograph by it if we heat it to incandescence.

Not only is it then light but all of the properties which make it available to us as iron have then gone out of it. It is as though the divine tapestry weaver had unwoven all the threads of the idea of iron and sorted them into their spectrum colors, thread by thread.

The physicist can tell you what element those threads

of light would be if frozen. Upon looking at them, he would say, "That is iron." But it would not be the form of iron as we know it—it would be the *formless idea of iron* as the sun knows it.

THERE IS NO SEPARATENESS

In the incandescent sun is all idea that earth knows. The idea of the apple of earth is in the sun, likewise the wood of the tree and the violet in the meadow. Likewise the cool earth is there, with its rivers and mountains.

All idea is one idea in the light of the sun. The light of the sun is never divided into its many seeming separate ideas until it is electrically extended from the sun and those extensions electrically echoed back to it.

The sun is a crucible which melts all ideas into one, then sets them out into space to cool and separate into many units of that one.

Likewise Idea of Mind never becomes the many ideas of Creation until electricity divides that One idea into many separate parts.

The One Light cannot be divided, but extensions of the One Light can appear to divide it. The spots of sunlight upon the cathedral floor are many, but they are all extensions of the one light of their source in the sun. Likewise all mankind is an extension of the One Idea of man for man is but One in the Light of his Source.

Likewise all moving extensions of the One still Light, as manifested in the white light of suns and the black light of their surrounding space, are but extensions of one Source.

ALL IDEA IS STILL

The cinema exemplifies this meaning. Upon the screen are many patterned ideas in noisy, violent motion. We know, however, that all of the motion of separate ideas, and all of the sounds emanating from those patterned, moving forms, would instantly cease if the still source of light from which these images and sounds are projected were turned off.

We know that the cause of all this transient division into positive and negative effect is in the one still light from which it is projected. We know that the sounds we hear emanate from that stillness, yet we seem to be totally unaware of the fact that all of our pulsing universe is but an extension of One still Light of Universal Mind, projected through positive and negative light upon the universal screen of space.

It is difficult to conceive earth and all of its phenomena of motion, sound, people, animals, and plant life, as a motion picture projection from our sun. Yet all of the separate ideas of earth are in that one incandescent light of the sun. All are but one thing, Light.

Turn off the sun and all of its patterned ideas on earth would instantly cease. The still idea which is extended into motion is not in the motion but in the stillness from which it is extended.

"For I say that man who senses but clay of earth in him is bound to earth as clayed image of his earth.

"Clayed images of My imagining who knoweth not Me in them are but dwellers of earth's dark. To sensed man the doors of My Kingdom are self-barred by darkness until the Light of Me in him is known by him as Me.

"Until then he is but moving clay, manifesting not Me in him while sensing naught but moving clay of him; knowing not the glory of My Light in him.

"Wherefore, I say to thee, exalt thou thyself beyond thy sensing. Know Me as fulcrum of thy thinking. Be Me as deep well of thy knowing."

—*From* THE DIVINE ILIAD

Chapter X

FUNCTION OF THE BRAIN

Electric awareness of observed effects of matter in motion is registered in the brain.

It is commonly believed that the brain thinks and knows.

The brain does not think, nor does it know. It is but a storehouse of recorded sensations. The brain "remembers" these records for man's usage as he needs them, and for fulfilling the requirements of his body.

The brain is a complex state of motion expressed by waves of light pulsing in cycles.

States of motion cannot KNOW anything, nor can they THINK anything.

The brain is part of a machine, a human machine.

Machines can express thoughts which are electrically projected through them, but machines are incapable of thinking the thoughts thus projected.

Likewise machines can express knowledge but they cannot have knowledge.

Likewise machines can do marvelous things when patterned and controlled by knowledge, but they cannot KNOW what they do.

FUNCTION OF THE BRAIN

The centering conscious Mind of man's Soul-will alone thinks by projecting desire for creative expression through the brain machine.

Desire in Mind is electrically expressed. Electricity is the motivative force which projects the One Light of Mind two ways to create cycles of light waves for the purpose of expressing thought cycles.

Desire is not in the brain. It is in the centering conscious self. *Desire is the cause of all motion.*

THE BRAIN RECORDS SENSATIONS

The brain is but the electric recording mechanism of conscious Mind thinking. It is also man's storage warehouse of electric records of memories and thoughts since his beginning.

It is the servant of Universal Intelligence. It operates all mechanisms of the body. It acts as the central switchboard for all its instinctive voluntary and involuntary actions.

The brain is the seat of sensation. Its purpose in this respect is to keep the body electrically informed of the condition of the body, through electrical messages.

Such messages are not mental. They are purely electrical. They produce sensation. The brain senses and records every message. It sends counteracting messages to other parts of the body.

The body is a vast and complex mechanism. The brain is an electrical recorder, distributor, broadcaster and receiver for all operational parts of that multi-celled machine, but its actions have no relation to intelligence.

The brain records sensations of experiences and observations which the senses convey to it. Such sensations are mistaken for thinking and knowing. Sensation arising from electrical motion is purely automatic.

The mistake in assuming that the brain thinks and knows is due to the fact that man believes himself to be thinking when he is only sensing. Man also believes that he is acquiring knowledge through sensed observation of sensed EFFECT, when he is but recording electrical sensations which inform him as to the nature of things observed by his senses.

The body is a patterned machine designed to do many things. Electric motivation through nerve wires determines each movement.

When such sensations act in unison with his conscious awareness of the Light which centers him as PERSON, he is then thinking as well as sensing.

The centering consciousness of man, the PERSON, transforms information received by the senses into knowledge to the extent of which he is capable of recognizing CAUSE in spirit, back of the EFFECT which his senses record.

Until that transformation takes place, man is without

knowledge no matter to what extent his senses may have informed him, for information is not knowledge.

A man may be a veritable encyclopedia of information. He may have earned many college degrees for being well informed and yet be without sufficient knowledge to create anything.

For instance, we cannot sense the idea of a harp while it is still, but we can know the idea of the harp. We can know its various possibilities of expression, even though its strings are not vibrating. Likewise we can imagine countless complexities of rhythms which lie unexpressed within those still strings.

Conversely, we cannot know the vibrations which come from those strings when we set them in motion. We can but sense those vibrations through our own sensed electrical awareness.

"The Source of all things is within all things, centering them as Rest, from which their motion springeth. It is also without all things, controlling their balance with all other things.

"Man's universe is still composed of many things, many separate things, and separable.

"Yea, not one thing is there in My imaged universe which is apart from Me, nor of itself alone.

"Yea, I guide My borning things from very seed by sensed threads of light extensions of My thinking until they themselves can guide themselves. Not e'en the least of these which are not bound to Me in Light.

"Images of My imaginings which grow from Earth, and those which freely move, all of these things grow and move through extended light of My dynamic thinking until they themselves can think with Me."

—*From* THE DIVINE ILIAD

Chapter XI

ELECTRICAL AWARENESS

This material universe of many seemingly separate parts is electric.

The whole universe of countless parts is wired together by an electric flux of "nerves" which inform each part of the universe of the ever changing condition of every other part.

There is no "sensation" between balanced parts or balanced conditions of matter. By "sensation" we mean the feel of the electric current which conveys the message. The electric current is impossible in an equilibrium condition, hence we can feel no sensation whatsoever when our bodies, or parts of them, are in a balanced condition.

Electrical awareness is necessary to an electrically mechanized universe. An electrically controlled machine in one's factory has exactly the same electric awareness that a man has. Its wired nervous system conveys electric messages to its parts for the dual purpose of motivating them as well as for adjusting all parts to each other in continuity.

Electric machines do what electric awareness

demands of them through sensation. So does man, tree, the solar system and every nebula of the heavens.

Man's body cells are electrically aware of their mechanistic purposes and respond to electric messages sent to them. They have electrical cell memory of their individual and group purposes. They act automatically when sensed reflexes are electrically motivated.

Bodily functions, such as our heartbeat, digestion, chemical gland transformation, breathing and walking, are automatically operated by cell memory reflexes.

Cell memory and instinct cause birds to migrate, spiders to spin webs and certain vegetable growths to close in on flies and fish.

Instinctive actions and cell memory reflex actions are not mental. They are purely mechanical and automatic.

ELECTRIC AWARENESS IS UNIVERSAL

This principle of electric awareness, through sensation, is not limited to animal life alone. It is equally characteristic of the mineral and vegetable kingdoms. It extends to the veriest electronic particle and to the mightiest galaxy.

Not only is each particle in each mass electrically aware of its purpose, but each particle in the entire universe reacts in response to electrical messages sent to it from every other particle in the universe. This physical universe is controlled solely by electrical sensation which is measured and balanced by the still magnetic Light, centering all things.

> *"For behold, saith the Universal One, I am within all things centering them; and I am without all things controlling them."*
>
> —*From* THE DIVINE ILIAD

All of the electric universe of motion is thus so perfectly conditioned by the two electric workers which build the universe and tear it apart sequentially for rebuilding, that all moving things in it sense all other moving things in it.

Likewise, all differently conditioned things in the universe readjust their conditioning to every change of condition of every other thing in the universe.

There is a constant separating process in Nature which forever expresses the universal desire for change and multiplicity, and there is likewise a constant levelling process which forever expresses the universal desire for oneness.

"I, with man, am creating man in My universal image.

"What I am, man is.

"I think idea; and the form of My idea appears in the pattern of My thinking.

"I think man; and man appears in the pattern of My thinking.

"Man thinks man; and man appears in the image of man's thinking.

"Man's thinking is My thinking.

"All thinking things are thinking My thinking.

"All creating things are formed in the image of My thought imaginings to manifest My thought imaginings.

"The universe is My image, creature of My imaginings."

—*From* THE DIVINE ILIAD

Chapter XII

INSTINCT

Organic matter generates purely from the desire of mind to manifest idea in matter. That cosmic desire to create form produces the desired form. Desire is the motivating force of all Creation.

Man begins to express the idea of man as a single cell. The whole idea of man is in that single cell. It then unfolds in orderly time and space according to cosmic law. Likewise the whole idea of all Creation is in that single cell. All idea is omnipresent. There are no parts of the Whole.

Each step in the unfolding of the man-idea follows the continuing desire for unfolding. Cell memory of purpose is given to each cell as it unfolds. Pattern of idea follows in sequence as desire in God Mind and desire in the growing idea work together to express the idea in form.

Every action of unfolding man is a part of the unfolding of the man-idea as it exists as a whole in God's Mind. Any desire of man is, therefore, a two-way extension of the Light of that idea from God to man. Whatever God desires to express in man He will express, for He is man's Creator.

Whatever man desires, the God in him will create. Man must, however, co-create with God according to God's universal law. If man breaks that law, the law will break him to an equal extent.

LIFE IS A SEQUENCE OF EXPERIENCES

All of the expressions of desire in the unfolding of any idea are a part of the idea. They are experiences in decisions. All experiences are parts of the unfolding of any idea.

Whatever those decisions are, however, they are recorded upon the individual man as his own interpretation of the man-idea. Likewise they are recorded in the whole of the race of man as the sum total of all desires and experiences of the whole man-idea.

As the idea of anything is one, so also the parts of that idea are one.

INSTINCTIVE INTERCOMMUNICATION

If it were not for instinct, animal life could not survive or develop.

Instinct causes mechanical actions to take place in all bodies to meet the necessities of existence. Instinct protects animal life from enemies. It tells the proper food to eat, how to build nests, how to take care of its young, how to return home when taken great distances, as the carrier pigeon does, and countless other wonderful things that animals do.

A salmon, spawned in a certain river, instinctively leaves that river and makes its way to the sea until maturity. At the proper time for its mating and spawning, it then returns, over thousands of trackless miles, to the very river in which it was born.

It is instinct which tells birds to fly south before winter. Instinct tells them the direction of south. Instinct tells them it is warmer in that direction. Instinct likewise governs the migration of seals, the building of the beaver's dam and the weaving of the spider's web.

Instinct might be defined as a cell-memory record of all actions of a body, and of all of the sensations caused by those actions.

THE BEGINNINGS OF INSTINCT

Without instinct in all animal and vegetable life, their evolution would not be possible. All creations of the Creator are the result of electric wave recordings of the Creator's thought. They are parts of the whole Idea taken apart and put together bit by bit. They are the result of Universal Law, of Cause and Effect.

None of the creations of the Creator have in them at their beginning the power to think. It takes millions of years for complex organisms to recognize the spirit within them sufficiently to think at all. During these long ages, they are guided almost entirely by their instinctive reflexes. Man alone has begun to think, reason, imagine, create and invent, and then only during the last few thousand years.

INSTINCT IS GOD-CONTROL

Instinct is, therefore, God-control over the actions of His creations. The involuntary actions of the body, such as the heartbeat, or the action of white corpuscles, do not know their purpose in the healing process of the body, but God centers and controls every atom of His Creation and each must fulfill its purpose.

INSTINCT BUILDING BY GOD AND MAN

A good example of the manner in which God and man work together for creative expression is the familiar knitting woman. Knitting is part of the man-idea which requires a skill. The woman who desires to knit must desire to acquire that skill. Desire must precede all expression of that desire.

Slowly she takes one stitch at a time. All of her power of concentration is needed to take those first stitches. Each stitch taken, however, has within it the desire for taking the next stitch.

Very slowly she interlaces yarns into the pattern required. The cells of her fingers gradually acquire cell memories of their purpose. These cells coordinate with other cells of the body in the development of the whole skill.

Gradually she learns to knit instinctively. Her mind is freed from concentration and she may think of other things and converse freely. Her body cells alone will work from the memory of purpose given to them.

Instinctive skills are thus imparted to bodies of man by the co-creative efforts of God and man. The pianist teaches his fingers to work instinctively in order to free his mind to think music. God is working with him. Without this moment-to-moment cooperation with God, he could do nothing.

God, Creator of all things, knows all things and has all power.

Man and God are One. Man may know all things and have all power to the extent in which he desires to know all things and have all power. Awareness of the Light in man will give him all knowledge and power. Man may not be apart from God at any time. Nor can any part of Creation be apart from God at any time.

"All things come and go from My divided thinking.

"All things go from very heart of Me into My imaged universe; and when they disappear from there I also take them back to very heart of Me.

"Know thou that all creating things are resurrected things, again manifesting life of Me through My divided thinking.

"Man divides his thinking in manifesting Me.

"The body of man sleeps, that it may awaken in Me, to manifest Me.

"The body of man dies, that it may be resurrected in Me, to manifest Me.

"The body of man disappears, that it may reappear to manifest Me.

"Man who sleeps or dies or disappears is but man's image, for Self of man sleeps not, nor dies, nor disappears; for Self of man is Me.

"Again I say that I am One, and man is One in Me when he knows that I am he."

—*From* THE DIVINE ILIAD

Chapter XIII

UNCONSCIOUSNESS, SLEEP AND PAIN

There is much confusion regarding the supposedly possible condition known as "being unconscious." When we sleep, or are anesthetized, we say we are "unconscious."

We cannot be unconscious. We have always been conscious without the slightest awareness of it.

Our confusion in this respect lies in mistaking sensation and thinking for consciousness.

When we stop thinking, whether asleep or awake, we do not stop KNOWING, nor do we cease being consciously aware of our Being. We but cease to set our knowledge in motion to express idea through the pulsations of thinking.

Conscious Mind does not sleep. Sleep is merely the negative half of the wave cycle of electrical awareness of sensation. Wakefulness is the positive half.

All nature sleeps when the sunlight lessens the ability of all things to manifest life. Sleep is the death half of the life-death cycle.

One may say, "I am unaware of this or that," but one cannot say "I am unconscious" when one is always conscious.

Conscious awareness is KNOWING. Unawareness means that one does not yet know. Knowledge is within him which he can know when he desires to know.

Sleep and wakefulness are positive-negative wave parts of a wave cycle, just as birth and death are opposite ends of a life cycle.

Sleep is but an anesthetic. Sleep can be induced chemically, either to the whole body or any part of it by desensitizing its cells. When the body or parts of it are thus "put to sleep," they have not been rendered "unconscious"; their voltage has merely been lowered.

The dentist does not refer to a local anesthetic as having produced unconsciousness; he refers to it as a desensitizing condition, but when the surgeon desensitizes the body, it is then supposed to be "unconscious." We assume that the brain has stopped thinking. The brain does not think, therefore it cannot stop doing that which it never does. We assume that bodies cease to be conscious, but consciousness is never in bodies.

A local anesthetic stops pain. Pain is a too intense electric current. The voltage is too great for the nerve wires to stand the strain. They burn out, and the overcharge of burning out causes the pain.

When the nerves of the body FEEL an electric current running through them, the body is aware that something is happening to throw it out of balance. When the body is in balance, it has no sensation. When the body is unbalanced, sensation informs it when and where, otherwise it could not function.

Wakefulness and sleep are merely the charging and discharging of the uncountable electric batteries of the body. If these batteries were kept constantly charged, there would be no such alternating conditions as sleep and wakefulness.

This planet is carrying us on our uphill journey to our pinnacle. The sun is the generator which charges its batteries. The sun is that generator, but the earth is turning toward and away from its generator continually.

As the sun's charging light disappears from one edge of the planet's rim at evening, everything goes to sleep. Conversely, all things awaken at the dawn. The batteries of all things on earth are being forever charged daily and discharged nightly.

"I center the moving shaft of My universe, yet I move not, although its power to move springeth from Me.

"I center growing systems, and changing cells of growing systems, yet I change not, e'en though their changing patterns spring from me.

"I center living things which manifest My life, but they live not. I alone live.

"Growing things are moving things in man's sensing, though they move not in man's knowing.

"Moving things are changing things in man's sensing, yet they change not in man's knowing.

"E'en though fast moving things of man's sensing move fast, they simulate the rest, while moving, from which they sprang into seeming motion."

—*From* THE DIVINE ILIAD

Chapter XIV

MOTION SIMULATING REST

This electric universe of motion forever moves to find rest, but never finds it. Matter in violent motion simulates rest and balance through violent motion. The more violent the motion the greater is the illusion of rest and balance. Motion can cease but it can never become rest.

THIS MAKE-BELIEVE UNIVERSE

The entire dynamic wave universe of electric matter is not what it seems to be. Everything which seems at rest depends upon violent motion to make believe it is at rest.

A wire wheel could appear to be a steel disk if spun fast enough. The faster it is spun, the more at rest it would seem.

This planet, seemingly at rest, is in violent motion around its centering point of rest from which it is electrically extended. Seemingly motionless clouds, floating above the earth, are rotating with it at the tremendous speed of one thousand miles an hour at the equator, or four times faster than a plane.

All the planets are revolving swiftly around their central sun which seemingly stands still in the heavens of space, but in fact is moving with incredible speed.

Likewise, all the stars of night, simulating rest, are moving at terrific speeds to adjust their mutual unbalances in this dual universe of divided pressure.

The pencil in one's hand, the desk upon which one is writing, the room full of motionless things, seeming to be at rest, are but simulating rest through violent motion of their many parts. Tremendous vibrations may be in that glass paperweight.

Not one thing could manifest the rest it simulates if it were not for the incredible speeds of those atoms which so incessantly rotate and revolve to make that seeming restfulness possible.

EVEN STILL THINGS ARE NOT STILL

All seemingly still matter is manifesting make-believe rest by make-believe motion.

Motion itself is an illusion. The motion one senses in one's brain has no more reality than the motion which one senses in a motion picture.

The seeming motion of the cinema is caused by sequences of changing patterned forms projected on the screen which give the impression of motion because of the rapid change of pattern in the negatives. That selfsame illusion applies to the material universe.

"Without change My play of Creation could not be played, nor its actors be. Behold, therefore, the changing universe of My imagining, the seeming universe of My thinking.

"And again I say that there is no change in Me, the changeless One, so, also, is there no change in My thought universe of pairs of opposed things which forever interchange to simulate My universe of change.

"E'en the seeming changing of My thought universe is not change save for senses of sensed things which are bound to pairs of parts of wholes.

"Each pair wendeth its way through the interchanging pressures of its electric journey. Each appeareth, then disappeareth, to reappear.

"E'en though senses of sensed things sense changing in all things, they change not to conscious knowing.

"Whyfor be thou slave to sensing? Rise above thy sensing. Be Me in thy knowing."

—*From* THE DIVINE ILIAD

Chapter XV

THE ILLUSION OF CHANGE

Change is an illusion of the senses due to motion.

There is no change whatsoever in the conscious universe of knowing. There is only an illusion of change set up by the two interchanging lights of thinking to divide the One Whole Idea into many separate ideas and record them in moving matter.

The senses are the audience for these thought pulsations. The senses are a part of this illusion. Senses are electric. They belong to the thought universe of motion and do not respond to stillness. As motion itself is non-existent, so also are senses non-existent.

The senses are but the imagined records of imagined motion, matter and change. As such they are limited to pin-hole peeks into the vastness which extends beyond their sensing. The senses have no knowledge of what they sense. They merely record motion.

The senses respond to motion in only one direction. They sense the forward flow of time but not its backward flow. If they could register both directions, they would become aware of the stillness of this zero universe of seeming motion.

The Universal One planned it this way, otherwise there could be no sequential manifestation of thought which constitutes the creating universe.

When our knowing exceeds our sensing, we will no longer be deceived by the illusions of our senses.

A man seeing a technicolor motion picture for the first time and without knowledge of such electric effects would think he were looking through a window at real happenings, unaware that it was but an illusion "created" by projecting positive light through patterned negatives. That is all that creation is; two lights projected through each other to simulate motion, form and change.

Our senses are like passengers on a fast-moving train. They sense parts of the landscape as they rush forward, while, to their senses, the landscape rushes backwards. The senses interpret these effects as matter in fast motion which is forever fast changing. A man, seeing the same train from a mountain, would sense that same fast motion and fast change as changeless and still.

As man unfolds from sensed man to spiritual man he gradually becomes aware of the two-way motion of all effect; that two ways being the visible effect which responds to his senses and the invisible effect which he knows but does not sense.

Gradually the time arrives in his unfolding when his full awareness of Cause voids all reliance upon sensation.

He then rises above his sensing. He then knows the universe of motion for what it is instead of for what it seems to be.

"See thou no more with outer eyes alone for thou hast knowing eyes to void the illusions of thy sensing.

"Throughout long aeons man hath walked his earth with eyes of outer seeing, giving belief to that earth of his body's sensing. Throughout his new aeons he must walk the earth of inner seeing and know Me in it as but visioning it in Light of Me and Light of him.

"For I think earth, and earth appeareth, disappeareth and reappeareth in balanced rhythms of My thinking. Wherefore, I say, man's earth and man are but My imagining, to come and go with My imagining. It is not Me, nor is it him; nor is it e'en what it seems to be to him.

"Nor shall man longer place earth before Me, gaining aught of earth and naught of Me.

"For I am a patient God. I patiently await awakening man.

"Awakening man is he who knoweth the Light of Me in him. Man may choose his own aeons for his awakening, but know Me he must. Until that day man's agony of unknowing shall be man's alone. His knowing must be his own desiring.

"Knowing man is ecstatic cosmic man. He who beginneth to know Me in him—yea, e'en him who suspecteth Me in him hasteneth his unfolding to cosmic man of all-knowing."

—*From* THE DIVINE ILIAD

Chapter XVI

THE SENSES DECEIVE

Imagine a perfectly motionless wheel and a fly walking around its rim, moving ever forward over changing ground, and the wheel seemingly moving backward, during a continuity of time in which the fly sensed a constant change in the changeless wheel.

Every time the fly got back to the same point, it would compute the past time consumed on the journey and the forward time necessary for the next circuit.

The wheel being still, motion, change and time are created by the fly itself as it takes the whole idea of the wheel apart by journeying around it and examining it bit by bit.

The fly sensed motion by changing its position on the wheel. It sensed change by finding a seeming difference of condition at each forward movement. It sensed time by creating the sequences necessary in taking the one idea of the wheel apart and dividing it into many separate ideas.

This simple analogy is a good symbol of Creation. This planet, like the fly on the wheel, moves forever around its motionless orbit. The orbit is as rigid and still as the wheel upon which the fly is moving.

As the planet moves upon the wheel of its orbit, it senses constant motion and change. It senses changes of days into nights, of spring merging into summer, autumn into winter. All of these seeming changes are in the motion of the planet and not in the wheel of its orbit. Each change is entirely due to the motion of the planet and not to the changeless orbit. The planet itself registers change on its changeless wheel. Change therefore lies in motion alone. The senses are motion, therefore the senses sense only that which they themselves are.

INADEQUACY OF THE SENSES

Man overrates his senses. He places too much dependence upon them without justification, for they are not recording all of the phenomena of his surroundings. He likewise trusts them too much without justification, for they are constantly deceiving him.

While his senses are recording the stillness and rest of Nature on a lazy afternoon, they are failing to record the violent motion of everything in his entire environment, from the blade of grass to the clouds in the heavens above him.

Those seemingly motionless clouds are moving at the speed of a thousand miles an hour at the equator without the slightest evidence of that swift motion being recorded upon his senses. The earth also is moving many miles per second in two directions; one of rotation upon its axis and the other of revolution around its orbit. His senses register stillness. They are electrically unaware of that motion.

This deception is as it should be, just as the same deception in a cinema is as it should be. God's universe is but an electric recording of His knowing, manifested by His thinking. To thus record the idea of His knowing in the two lights of His thinking, a three dimensional universe is necessary. If the senses could detect and record all motion, instead of but a part of it, the illusion would disappear. The senses would see behind the illusion and find that all motion voids itself. Division of the whole into parts causes the illusion. If the film were removed from the projector of the motion picture, the illusion of motion and change would be voided.

That is what Creation is, the One Light of knowing divided into the patterned parts of thinking. Sensing is but an electric tension set up by the seeming division of one into many which "strain" to fulfill their desire for oneness.

When a unity of condition is consummated, sensation between those parts ceases because the tension ceases. The senses, being but tension of desire for unity between divided parts, have no existence.

The senses are electric flux threads of light connecting every particle in the universe with every other particle.

They are the intercommunicating nerves of the one universal body.

When strain of desire for balance, rest or unity ceases, sensation ceases.

In this electric universe, sensation is the strain of resistance to the separation which exists between all separated masses. All matter is one. Separated particles desire to find that oneness.

It is part of God's plan that the senses are limited entirely to the recording of a very small fraction of effect. The senses can never sense the Whole but the conscious Mind can KNOW the Whole.

"These words I now say for newly comprehending man of his new cycle.

"Love ye one another all men; for ye are one in Me.

"Whatsoe'er ye do to one in Me ye do to all; for all are one in Me.

"Love thy brother as thy self. Serve thy brother before thy self. Lift high thy brother, lift him to high pinnacles, for thy brother is thy self.

"For of a verity, I say, love of self, or nation of selves, turneth neighbor against neighbor, and nation against nation. Self love breeds hate and soweth its seed in all the winds to blow where'er it will. Wherefore say I, love of neighbor for neighbor, and nation for nation, uniteth all men as one.

"Serve first thy brother. Hurt first thy self rather than thy neighbor. Gain naught from him unbalanced by thy giving. Protect thou the weak with thy strength, for if thou use thy strength against him his weakness will prevail against thee, and thy strength will avail thee naught.

"He who giveth love prospereth mightily; but he who taketh aught gaineth naught.

"Whyfor lose all to gain the world, gaining naught?

"He who hath not laid up a treasure in heaven to equal treasure gained of earth has sought the dark.

"For him the Light is far."

—*From* THE DIVINE ILIAD

Chapter XVII

MAN'S NEW CYCLE

This coming age will mark an epochal advancement in man's evolution toward his goal of omniscience and omnipotence.

Man becomes a higher being with greater power as he acquires knowledge. In knowledge alone lies power. Only through knowledge can man become co-creator with God.

Knowledge can be obtained by man only through awareness of the Spirit within him. Lack of that awareness is the tragedy of today's civilization.

During the last century of the greatest scientific progress in the history of man, great nations of the world have killed, robbed, and enslaved other men to build their own empires.

Even today man kills by the millions, condoning his killing as necessary for his self-preservation. He is now but reaping the seed of his sowing. He who lives by the sword shall die by the sword.

No man can hurt another man without condemning himself to greater hurt.

Fear dominates the world of today. *While fear is in the*

world love cannot also be. Love can never dominate the world until man ceases to live a primarily sensed existence and knows the Light of the spirit within him.

This new age brings man one step nearer to the universe of greater knowing through greater comprehension of man's relation to man, and to God.

Each past cycle in the growth of man toward higher levels has been illumined by the few inspired messengers of the Light who have known God in themselves.

New inspired messengers who know God in themselves will likewise give the Light to this new cycle. And these few messengers of the Light must multiply into legions, for the need of a spiritual awakening is great.

Man's whole reason for being is to gradually pass through his millions of years of physical sensing into his ultimate goal of spiritual knowing. Man has now reached a transition point in his unfolding where he must have that knowing. He can acquire that knowing only through greater awareness of the Light of the universal Self which centers him as One with God.

THE SECRET OF LIGHT

Part II

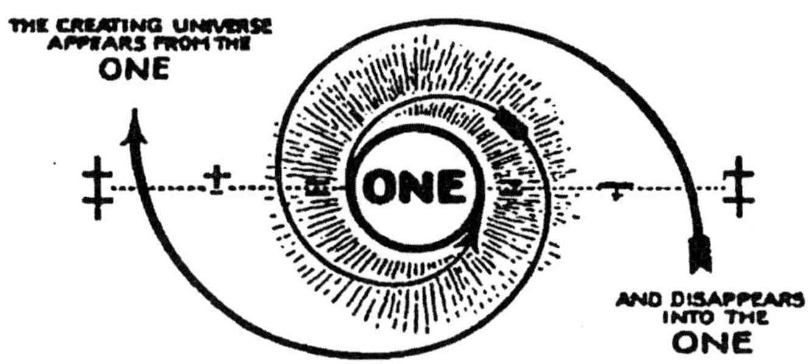

OMNIPOTENCE

The Universe of Power

"Without thinking My One Idea could not become many one ideas for My stage setting.

"Without motion My cosmic play could not be played, nor could its actors be.

"Without change my undivided One Idea could not unfold.

"Without time My drama of My creating universe could have no sequences.

"Without motion, time, change and sequences the unfolding of My Mind imaginings could have no measured space for its stage settings, no screen for its light projections.

"Therefore see them as I imagine them; but know that they are but unfolding patterns of My knowing through My thinking.

"Know thou, therefore, that time is naught, nor are there moving things which change; nor is there life, nor death, nor cold, nor heat, nor good, nor bad in My universe of Me."

—*From* THE DIVINE ILIAD

Chapter I

MAN'S TWO SUPREME ILLUSIONS

The secret of Light is fathomable to man only by first solving his two supreme illusions. The greater of these is the illusion of the universe itself. Man has never known his universe for what it really is, but only for what his senses have made him believe it to be. His senses have deceived him mightily.

The other is the illusion of man himself. With the exception of the Nazarene, man has never as yet known man. Nor has he known his relation to the universe, nor to his still more unfathomable God.

The little that man knows of himself and his universe is what the eyes and ears of his body have told him they have seen and heard about himself and his universe.

But man has eyes and ears of the spirit which see and hear what man's sensed eyes and ears can never see or hear, for man is still too new in his unfolding. He is still but in the ferment of his beginnings.

Man senses motion, change, sequence, multiplicity,

time, activity, life, death, good and evil. Of these things he is most certain. His senses have made him most certain of their substantial reality. In face of the fact that he has lived with his familiar universe all his life, it is not easy for him to accept the statement that it has no existence whatsoever, that it is all illusion, all of it, nothing being left upon which to even base that illusion.

He can accept the illusion of the railroad tracks meeting upon the horizon, but the railroad tracks are real, even though their seeming meeting is not. They, at least, still remain as a basis for their own illusion.

A mirage of a city is comprehensible to man also as an illusion. He knows it does not exist but he also knows of the reality of the city which thus repeats itself, ghostlike, in the mirrors and lenses of light waves of the heavens above the city. To tell him that the city, as well as its own mirage, has no existence is to lay too heavy a tax upon his credulity and patience.

Yet that is what the secret of Light reveals, and that is what we must tell, simply and convincingly, to layman, churchman and scientist alike, and in the language standards and methods which each requires for his conviction.

So come, therefore, and know God, His universe, and man with eyes other than our sensed ones. The eyes of the spirit are knowing eyes. God's universe of knowing is all that is. The universe of seeming motion does not exist.

"Whyfor be thou slave to sensing. Be Me in thy knowing."

—*From* THE DIVINE ILIAD

"The heavens and the earths of My curved universe are father-mother of My universe, each of each and each to the other one. Neither one can be save the other also be.

"Nor can one leave the other, saying, 'Sit thou here while I journey to the far reaches.'

"Nor can there be aught upon the earth without the fathering skies, nor in the skies without the motherhood of earth; neither man, nor bird, nor reptile, nor fish, nor beast of wild jungle; neither tree, nor flower, nor shrilly singing insect; neither tempest, wild tornado, nor gentle breeze of calm ocean; nor cloud, nor mist, nor dewdrop for flower petal; not one of these things can be born of earth alone unfathered by the heavens, nor can heaven alone born them without the motherhood of earth.

. . "Again I say: I, the Light, am One. But my thinking is two, for thought is two in every creating thing, two halves of One which never can be one. Always must they be two to go opposed ways from Me and back again to Me for reborning from the other one after finding rest in Me."

—*From* THE DIVINE ILIAD

Chapter II

GENESIS

I

In the beginning God, the Father.

The Father is Light, the still Light of the Spirit Whom no man can see.

The dwelling place of the Father is the kingdom of Heaven; and it is without form and void.

In the Light is the seed of Creation; and the Light is Father of the seed. In the Light is Being, and in the seed is desire for Being. And desire in the seed is soul in the seed.

The Father in Heaven knows His Idea. He knows it as One, the undivided One.

In the Father Light is the seed of all-knowing. In Him is two-fold desire to unfold and refold His seed of all-knowing into imaged forms of His imagining, by dividing wholeness into parts, stillness into motion, unchanging into changing, unconditioned into conditioned, void into form, infinity into measure, eternity into time and immortality into mortality.

II

The spirit of God moved to fulfill His two desires and said: "Let there be Light; and let darkness shine out of Light and Light out of darkness." And it was so.

The One Light of the Father in His Kingdom of Heaven divided the void. And behold, two father-mother lights of nightless suns shone out of the darkness of the void and day appeared in undivided oneness of everlasting day.

And the Father centered His suns as seed of His desire that forms should appear from formless Light to fulfill His desire for division of the One into many divided ones formed in the image of His imagining.

And mighty polar breathings of desire within the nightless suns begat earths to course suns' far heavens to divide the day and give night to day to mate the day. And lo! night was born on earths from nightless day and day was born from night.

And God saw that it was good that each of the two, begat from One, was born of each other, to disappear into the One, to reappear as the other.

Thus the One Light of God's knowing extended to the two of His thinking, pulsed as the three of all creating things, the One centering the two, the two extended from the One; the Spirit; the Father-Mother polarity of Light; the Trinity centering the shaft of Creations' seeming, fulcrum of its heartbeat, all ONE.

III

The manner of the extension of God's knowing to His thinking was in this wise:

The Father of the kingdom extended His arms of still Light unto His heaven and said to one: "Sit thou here and look thou inward. Be thou seed of My knowing for repeating My thinking. Refold thou the forms of My imagining within thy stillness and give them back to Me for resurrection in the imaged forms of My imagining.

"Father thou My thinking; and let thy name be North, for North, in Light, means inward breathing from the heavens toward oneness in the seed. Guide thou the enfolding forms of My imagining from seed of thee to centering seed of Me."

And to the other Light the centering Spirit said: "Sit thou here and look thou outward. Be thou womb of My knowing for borning My thinking. Unfold thou My seed from the stillness of seed and give earth forms of them to heavens to manifest Me.

"Mother thou My thinking; and let thy name be South, for South in Light means outward breathing from the seed into their heavens. Interweave thou thy threads of light of earths and suns with threads of light from heavens into patterns of My thinking extended from My knowing to manifest My knowing."

IV

To North and South the Father said: "Behold in Thee and Me the firmament of my desiring to mirror the Light of My knowing into father-mother forms of My imagining."

And earths appeared below and heavens above the firmament, each being each, each mirrored from the other to become the other.

And lo! all imaginings in seed of earths unfolded into the heavens for heaven's refolding into patterned seed of earths for earth's reborning; and behold, God's imaginings pulsed with life of His imaginings within His omnipresent kingdom.

In this wise God divided the waters from the waters: those which were under the firmament from those which were above the firmament, and each was of each, and each of the other.

And God saw that it was good. All things were thus divided, as two halves of one which never could be one, but must forever born the other from each other to manifest the Knowing of the One as the two opposed desires of His thinking.

V

And all-knowing was in the Light. And God sowed seed-suns of all-knowing Light unto far reaches of His firmament for borning into patterned images of His imagining.

"And the earth brought forth grass, and herb yielding seed after his kind, and the tree yielding fruit, whose seed was in itself, after his kind: and God saw that it was good." (GENESIS 1:12)

"And God said, Let the waters bring forth abundantly the moving creature that hath life, and fowl that may fly above the earth in the open firmament of heaven.

"And God created great whales, and every living creature that moveth, which the waters brought forth abundantly, after their kind, and every winged fowl after his kind: and God saw that it was good."

"And God blessed them, saying, Be fruitful, and multiply, and fill the waters in the seas; and let fowl multiply in the earth." (GENESIS 1:20, 22)

"And God said, Let the earth bring forth the living creature after his kind, cattle, and creeping thing, and beast of the earth after his kind: and it was so.

"And God made the beast of the earth after his kind, and cattle after their kind, and every thing that creepeth upon the earth after his kind: and God saw that it was good." (GENESIS 1:24 and 25)

VI

And it was that God had whispered to man for long ages while man was new, but man heard not God's whispering.

And God said, "Let us give man knowing and make him in our image after our likeness; and let him have 'dominion over the fish of the sea, and over the fowl of the air, and over the cattle, and over all the earth, and over every creeping thing that creepeth upon the earth.'" (GENESIS 1:26)

And lo, man knew God in him and emerged from the dark of his jungle into dawn of the Light in him and turned his eyes upward toward the Mount of his ascension from sensing to knowing. And man desired his ascension to the Light.

And God saw that it was good and dwelt within man to give him the Light of all-knowing, as awakening man desired the Light of all-knowing.

"Great art is simple. My universe is great art, for it is simple.

"Great art is balanced. My universe is consummate art, for it is balanced simplicity.

"My universe is one in which many things have majestic measure; and again another many have measure too fine for sensing.

"Yet I have not one law for majestic things, and another law for things which are beyond the sensing.

"I have but one law for all My opposed pairs of creating things; and that law needs but one word to spell it out, so hear Me when I

say that the one word of My one law is

BALANCE

"And if man needs two words to aid him in his knowing of the workings of that law, those two words are

BALANCED INTERCHANGE

"If man still needs more words to aid his knowing of My one law, give to him another one, and let those three words be

RHYTHMIC BALANCED INTERCHANGE"

—*From* THE DIVINE ILIAD

Chapter III

THE LAW OF BALANCE

The underlying law of Creation is RHYTHMIC BALANCED INTERCHANGE in all transactions in Nature. It is the one principle upon which the continuity of the universe depends. Likewise, it is the one principle upon which the continuity of man's transactions, his health and happiness depend. It is the manifestation of God's two opposing desires in all processes of creation.

BALANCE is the principle of unity, of oneness. In it is the stability which lies in CAUSE. Balance is the foundation of the universe.

BALANCED INTERCHANGE simulates oneness by interchange between pairs of opposites. It is the principle of equal giving between all moving pairs of unbalanced opposites which constitute this dual electric universe. In it is the instability of EFFECT. Instability is forever seeking to find stability. It can never find it, but it can simulate it by balancing its instability through equality of interchange.

RHYTHMIC BALANCED INTERCHANGE is the principle of continuity of EFFECT *Balanced inter-*

change between opposites repeats simulation of stability, and *rhythmic* balanced interchange continues that repetition.

OBEDIENCE TO THE ONE LAW IS ABSOLUTE

Rhythmic balanced interchange is the inviolate law which must be obeyed. Nature persistently violates it and Nature instantly pays the price of its violations in its storms, tornadoes, crashing avalanche and tragedy of field, forest and jungle.

Man persistently violates it and instantly pays the price of his violation in his crashing business failures, enmities, unhappiness and illness.

All the storms of earth cannot affect the balance of the earth, for balance in the universe cannot be upset. The earth continues in its fixed, balanced orbit with so much precision that its position can be determined at any time to the split second.

If the earth disobeyed this law by the slightest variance, its oceans would sweep its continents clear of all living and growing things.

MAN MUST PAY FOR DISOBEDIENCE

Man's disobedience to the law cannot affect the balance of man in his whole journey, for every unbalanced action of his must eventually be balanced. Man is on his way to his cosmic goal of Oneness with his Creator and he can in no way deviate from that fixed orbit which will eventually take him to his destination of glory in the high heavens. By disobeying the law he is but hurting himself while on his journey, but he must make the journey and must balance every unbalanced action while on the way.

It is as though a man on a great ocean liner disobeyed the laws of the ship. In spite of his disobedience the ship is taking him to his destination and he must go with it. Likewise, he has hurt himself by lessening the happiness of his journey.

The whole principle of Creation lies in equal giving. The Oneness of the Light is divided into an equal and opposite two, and all interchange between the two must be equal in their giving.

God's division of the Light into a seeming two is manifested in Nature by electric waves of two opposing lights springing from the still sea of God's magnetic Light, just as waves of water spring from the still ocean.

The outstanding characteristic of waves is that they forever interchange. Troughs become crests and crests become troughs. Gravity pressure above and below their axis is equal. So long as equality of interchange continues rhythmically, waves repeat their interchange. When the sloping sand at the beach prevents this equality of rhythmic balanced interchange, the waves accumulate unbalance until they crash on the shore.

Every transaction in human relations either continues or discontinues in accord with obedience or disobedience to this one law. A man who sells and gives less value for what is given to him lays the foundation for his own wreckage. He finds it ever harder to sell and loses many purchasers by gaining their ill will. He who gives equally for what is given to him multiplies his purchasers and prospers by gaining their good will.

The pulse beat, the swinging pendulum, the inbreathing and outbreathing of living things all exemplify God's one law of rhythmic balanced interchange. Any deviation from that law in the heart-beat of a man would endanger his continuance, but when there is a rhythmic balanced interchange between the two compression and expansion opposites, man's life continues to function at maximum.

Man has free right to choose his own actions, but he must balance those actions with equal and opposite reactions until he learns that God's one law must be obeyed. This God holds inviolate.

The whole purpose of life is to learn how to manifest God in Truth and the Law. The lesson is a hard one but man, himself, makes it hard by his unknowing of the law. As man gradually knows his purpose and the law by knowing God in him, life becomes more and more beautiful, and man more powerful in his manifestation of power.

Man's power lies in giving. He must learn to give as Nature gives. Each half of a cycle eternally gives to the other half for re-giving. Nature forever unfolds into many for the purpose of refolding into one. Each individual must manifest this universal law.

The desire of some so-called "apron string" parents to run their children's lives for them, often claiming that they have sacrificed their very own lives for them, are *taking* from their children—not *giving*. They are taking away the initiative children need to complete their own cycles: they must live their own lives for themselves.

Man must know the principle of Creation: giving between each interchanging opposite half of each cycle for the purpose of repeating its giving. This is universal law and each individual must manifest this law.

Man will forever war with man until he learns to give his all with the full expectation of equal receiving, and never taking that which is not given as an earned reward for his giving.

"All things are One, but made to appear as two extensions of the centered One.

"Know thou that the two extensions of My recorded thinking are divided by the One which centers the two, the One balancing the two, the One controlling the two.

"I, the One, am not divided into two, as pairs of opposites of Me. I divide the two extensions of My thinking but I am not My thinking, nor am I two.

"When man thinketh man alone, denying Me, then is man's image man's, not Mine and man's, for the pattern of My balanced, rhythmic images within man may not be seen in him; nor may the glory of My Light be seen in him or known by him.

"When man thinketh Me, through knowing Me, then is he patterned by My image and I am he.

"When man thinketh Me in him, then is man's balance absolute.

"When man so thinketh, then hath he all power that I, thy Father-Mother-Thinker of Creation hath."

—*From* THE DIVINE ILIAD

Chapter IV

THE SOURCE OF POWER

God, the Creator, is POWER. There is no other power. All energy lies within the stillness of the One Magnetic Light of God.

God is Mind, the Intelligence of the universe. In God's Mind is One Idea, which God knows as One Whole Idea.

In God's Mind is desire to give creative expression to that One Idea by thinking it into parts. Desire in the Light of Mind is the *power* quality of Mind. Desire is the *soul* of Mind; the *will* of Mind.

God expresses the desire of Mind to manifest His Idea by creating this electric wave universe.

This electric universe is the sole product of God's Mind.

All product of God or man is the result of desire of Mind to create product.

The power to create product is in Mind. It is not in the product. Product has no power in itself to produce itself.

This assumption that product has power within itself to produce itself is another of man's illusions which have deceived the senses of man during these early days of his unfolding. It is as though the architect gave to his cathedral the power of creating itself.

The cathedral is an expression of desire of the architect to give form to the idea of his knowing. The power to create the idea is in the knowing. The idea of the cathedral already exists. The eyes of the spirit can see its spiritual image as clearly as the eyes of the body can sense it in stone as product of his knowing.

The expression of power to create the idea as product—lies in the electric action of thinking idea at rest in the Light of Mind into the two lights of waves of motion which simulate that idea.

As servant of Mind, electricity gives moving form to the idea by performing the work necessary to produce it. The power to thus produce does not lie in electricity nor in motion. *It lies in desire of Mind only. Without that desire Creation could not be. Without desire of Mind in man his power to create could not be.*

Mind is Light at rest. Desire of Mind is expressed through waves of light in motion. The expression of power in waves is not power. All of the power of the ocean is in its stillness, whether expressed or not. Likewise all of the power of Light is in the stillness of its knowing whether expressed by light waves or not.

All expressions of energy spring from rest, seek a point of rest and return to a condition of rest. The power of a moving lever is not in the lever nor in its motion. It is in the stillness of its fulcrum from which it borrows its ability to manifest the power of its fulcrum.

God is the fulcrum of man, and of the universe. Neither man nor any moving thing in the universe, has power within himself to do anything. All power expressed by man must be extended directly from the Father in heaven to His father-mother lights of earths and heavens which manifest Him.

The mechanical principle by means of which power is expressed by the Creator is in the light waves of two-way motion which record His two-way thinking. Waves are two-way cycles which are divided equally to express the two desires of Mind to create form images of Mind imagining and to destroy those forms sequentially for reforming.

Waves of motion spring from the stillness of the universal equilibrium. They are the universal heartbeat which manifests eternal life and power in God's stillness by eternal repetitions of simulated life and power as expressed in waves of motion.

Waves of motion express the power of desire for unbalance and motion which is in Light at rest, and they also express the opposite desire for balance and rest which is in motion.

Desire in the One Light of Mind is positive. Its expression in the two lights of opposed motion is negative. Every expression of power in Nature is negated by its opposite expression.

The senses are limited to the perception of but one of these negations at a time, and then only in small fractions of whole cycles. If the senses could record the whole of each cycle both ways, they would record stillness, not motion, for every action would be voided by its oppositely flowing reaction.

"For I have ordained that the father-mother of My imaged stage, its players and its motions become an equal two extension-retraction of My Light.

"An equal two must be an equal two, for desire of each to outbalance each would upset My spatial stage and all the father-mother offspring of My stage.

"Therefore, I have set a measure in My high heavens to balance each with each, that each might have its all, but not one whit more; nor lose aught, nor gain one whit more.

"Wherefore I, the ONE, watch o'er all My creating pairs of father-mothered things with My two measuring eyes to balance that which fathers My universe with that which mothers it.

"And as My sexed electric universe is two, so also must its watchful measuring eyes be two, centered by another One from which the two extend and seem to move as that mirage expression of My thinking seems to move."

—*From* THE DIVINE ILIAD

Chapter V

THIS SEXED ELECTRIC UNIVERSE

The still magnetic Light of the Father of all Creation is One. The One Light is the positive principle. It is CAUSE.

The moving electric father-mother lights of all Creation are two. The two are opposites of each other. The two negate each other. They are the intercommunicating nerves of the universal body, like those of man's body through which he senses things. They have not existence save an awareness of each other. They are but mirage extensions of Mind imagining which senses that which they but manifest.

Each electric opposite conditions the other with sex unbalance. Each sexed condition gives unbalance to the other to separate each from each to increase the power of each to oppose each. Each then gives of itself to the other to void the unbalanced condition of each other. In order to effect balance in each, each must become the other. The charging one must discharge and the discharged one must charge. Voidance of unbalance can only come that way. Likewise repetition can come only that way.

The electric universe is the negative principle. It is EFFECT. The two moving lights of the electric universe are two equal halves which express themselves in opposite directions. Their sole purpose is to oppose.

Opposites which violently oppose and void each other can never become one, nor can they attract each other.

SEX DEFINED

Sex is the division of a balanced equilibrium condition into two equally unbalanced conditions which negate each other periodically for the purpose of repeating the two unbalanced conditions.

Sex is the creative principle. It is the dual *desire* force in Mind for expressing its One Idea. Without a division of the one unconditioned Light into two seemingly conditioned lights, Creation could not be.

Sex is not a *thing,* it is a *condition* of a thing.

An electrically balanced condition of anything is sexless whether it be a man, woman, electric battery, or the atmosphere.

A sexed condition is an unbalanced condition. An electric battery which is fully charged is dually unbalanced by the opposite electric pressures of compression and expansion. These two opposite unbalanced conditions violently desire to return to the oneness of balance from which they were divided into two. A short circuit between the two poles of the battery will give it that balance. We then say it is dead, for it will no longer perform work by expressing its desire for balance.

An unbalanced atmosphere will violently seek a balanced condition, depending upon the intensity of the unbalanced condition. When calm follows the storm, it means that desire for balance has gone out of it, for when balance has been attained by rest, motion is no longer possible.

The sexed condition of unbalance in man is exactly the same in all phenomena in Nature. An unbalanced sex condition in man demands balancing in the same way, and its violence depends upon its electrical measure of unbalance. When that desire is satisfied and balance is restored, man is as sexless as the dead storage battery and for the same reason.

Man is recharged into a sexed condition by his heartbeat, by the food he eats and by his inbreathing-outbreathing. These are the generators which recharge the "dead storage batteries" of all the universe into sexed conditioned "live batteries."

A sexed condition and an electric condition are identical. Electricity conditions all sexless matter into its sexed condition, by dividing a pressureless condition into two opposite pressures which desire release from their opposition. All of the work of the universe is performed as a result of that desire in unbalanced matter to seek rest in a balanced condition.

This is a sexed electric universe in every effect of motion, whether it be in the heart of a giant sun or in the petal of a meadow violet.

Every action of motion in the universe is a result of sex desire for motion from a state of rest, or for rest from a state of motion.

These two sex desires of electric action and reaction are the result of the two desires of the Father to manifest His One Light through the extended father-mother lights which interweave His idea of Creation into the multiple forms of that idea and void them periodically for the purpose of repeating them.

The desire for two-way motion in equal action and reaction is reflected in the dual electric desire to give for regiving, and to unfold for refolding.

"Each thing in My universe is paired as opposite expressions of that thing. Neither expression is that which it expresseth; therefore, both life and death of things which seem to live and die, are neither life nor death.

"For all things in My universe interchange with their opposites and with all other things.

"Each opposite becometh the other sequentially, for, I say, in Me is Balance. I balance all opposites of pairs of things with equal opposites of pairs of things."

—*From* THE DIVINE ILIAD

Chapter VI

SEX-CONDITIONED OPPOSITES

The entirety of this balanced universe is thus divided into unbalanced pairs of father-mother sex-conditioned sex mates for the purpose of seemingly dividing universal Oneness into a universe of many ones.

No matter what names we use to designate one pair of sex mates from another, whether gravity and radiativity, male and female, positive and negative, charge and discharge, centripetal and centrifugal, generative and radiative, integrative and disintegrative, plus and minus, heat and cold, life and death, buyer and seller, producer and consumer, import and export, emptying and filling, inward and outward, north and south, heaven and earth, growth and decay—all of them are similarly conditioned by the two opposite electrical conditioners.

In other words, they are all being either compressed or expanded if we use pressure terms; or charged and discharged if we use electrical terms. Both are the same. Likewise, all that are being compressed or charged by positive electricity are simultaneously being expanded and discharged by negative electricity to a lesser extent.

Likewise, all that are being expanded by negative electricity are simultaneously being compressed and charged by positive electricity to a lesser extent. This is a two-way universe in all effects of motion, and both opposite effects are expressed in both mates simultaneously as well as sequentially.

THIS TWO-WAY UNIVERSE

Electricity is forever winding light up into hot spheres, surrounded by cold cube wave-fields of space, and likewise sequentially unwinding them for rewinding. While winding them into compressed light masses, they are simultaneously unwinding to a lesser extent. Conversely, while unwinding they are simultaneously rewinding to a lesser extent.

Every opposite of a pair charges in excess of its discharge for one half of its cycle. It then discharges in excess of its charging. Life and death are good examples. Life charges a body in excess of its discharge for one half of its cycle and death discharges it in excess for the other half.

Likewise the sun charges the earth during half of its twenty-four hour cycle in excess of its charge on the night side of the planet. The night side sequentially becomes the day side. The discharge of night then reverses to a preponderance of charge.

SEX-CONDITIONED OPPOSITE

The father-mother principle is fundamental in every expression and both are simultaneously manifested in every expression, each being preponderant sequentially during half of each cycle.

The father principle multiplies light into density and high potential. The mother principle divides it into vapors and gases of lower potential. Light is thus multiplied and divided into suns and planets surrounded by "space."

The "matter" of earth is the same as the matter of heavens with but one difference; VOLUME. And therein lies the secret of the universal pulse beat. Space is a division of solidity into tenuity. It is also a multiplication of volume at the expense of potential. Interchange between these two unbalanced opposites is the basis of all motion in this rhythmic universe.

Sex mates are two equal halves of one. They never can be one. They can never unite for they are the opposites of motion. Opposites of motion can cease to be and by thus ceasing to be they can give birth to the other opposite, but they never can be other than opposite.

OPPOSITES BORN EACH OTHER

Compression can never expand but expansion is born from compression. Conversely, expansion can never compress, but compression is born from expansion.

They can interchange with their opposites with every pulse beat, and they do. Each opposite is born from the other. Each pulse beat brings each opposite nearer to voidance of each and complete interchange into the other. It becomes the other sequentially at the halfway point in its cycle, but it is still an opposite. Opposites oppose. They never perform any other office than to oppose.

Opposition alone produces the idea of separateness in a universe of one inseparable thing.

The opposite of water is water vapor. Water is a compressed condition. It is of the father-light. Water vapor is the expanded condition of water. It is of the mother-light. They are two halves of one which never can be one.

The mother-light unfolds from the father-light. The father-light refolds the water vapor into water. Each has been born from the other. Each IS the other but they can never unite to become one.

All idea of Mind is thus divided into sex pairs of opposite mates. Matter is divided into solids and gases. The gases are the solids outwardly bound toward the heavens. Solids are those same gases inwardly bound toward gravity.

Heat and cold are opposites. Inwardly bound light rays generate heat from cold by compressing cold. Outwardly bound light rays degenerate heat into cold by expanding heat. It is said that cold is less heat. One might as well say that east is less west. East and west are two opposites just as cold and heat are opposites.

OPPOSITE SEX CONDITIONS BORN EACH OTHER

Matter and space likewise are sex mates. Each has become what each is by opposing the other to attain the appearance of separateness. Then each interchanges with each by breathing into and out of each other until space disintegrates matter and becomes what the other was. Space disintegrates suns and earths by the way of equators and generates them by the way of poles. Heat generated by cold by the way of poles is radiated by the way of equators. Suns thus turn inside-out. Cold bores black holes right through their poles and great suns become rings, like those in Lyra and other ring nebulae which are plentiful in the heavens.

All matter is generated by the degeneration of its opposite. Likewise all generated matter is sequentially degenerated by the generation of its opposite.

Compression in matter is balanced by an equal evacuation in space. Every unbalanced condition in Nature must be balanced by an equal opposite. All borrowings from the bank of Nature are debited with an amount equal to the credit extended just as money borrowed from man's bank is debited and credited.

DESIRE FOR REST FOLLOWS DESIRE FOR MOTION

The two are always two and never can become one, although the desire for oneness is with each during the entirety of its cycle. It is this desire for oneness which causes them to interchange. When credits and debits are balanced by interchange with each other, they cease to be. They do not become one.

When electrical opposites thus cancel each other out by interchange of their plus and minus conditions, they do not *neutralize* each other, as commonly believed—they cease to be.

MOTION CANNOT BE NEUTRALIZED

There is no exception to this process of Nature. All idea is recorded electrically in equal pairs of opposite expressions. Each of the pair cancels the other out in cyclic periodicities. Each then becomes what the other was.

Generation of any idea exceeds radiation during the first half of its cycle. Radiation then exceeds generation for the second half of the cycle. Both of these simulations of the idea, as expressed by motion, disappear. The idea still exists, however. The idea is at rest in its seed from which it can again appear in form of idea.

The two points of rest which are the fundamentals of every cycle are: the point of beginning at the wave axis, and the point of interchange between positive and negative opposites at the wave amplitude.

At these two rest points, motion has utterly ceased. It has not been *neutralized* into a condition of rest.

"The One Light of Me desires to be two. Two sensed warring divisions of the One spring forth from My unsensed Oneness into an imaged space. Two voiding lights of My One White Light spring from their Rest in unity to find rests of their own, but find not two but one, for two rests there cannot be in My universe of One.

"For I say that each light seeks rest in each where wave of My pulsed thinking meets wave, and at that mutual point of rest each voids each in the One from which another two spring into their mirrored infinities.

"Hear thou Me when I say that all things which flow from Me are sex-conditioned pairs of two, even to the cosmic dust of space which formeth new worlds, yea, and even to the heart of blazing fires of hottest suns.

"Naught is there in My divided universe which is not sex-conditioned, sex-interchanging and sex-balancing. Thus these moving pairs seek balance in voidance forever to repeat the thought-patterns of My thinking in the sex-balancing voidance of their 'conditioning.'"

—*From* THE DIVINE ILIAD

Chapter VII

THE SEX REPRODUCTIVE PRINCIPLE

All creating things are paired as unbalanced equal and opposite sex mates.

Reproduction of two unbalanced mates cannot be repeated until balance has first been restored. The calm surface of the ocean may be broken up into waves, but those waves cannot be repeated until the calm surface of the ocean has been restored to the equilibrium of its rest position, even though that rest position is not maintained.

Reproduction begins at the rest point where the previous wave cycle ends. Reproduction of unbalance must find a fulcrum from which the wave lever may leap into wave expression for repetition of pattern. That is what Creation is, merely the repetition of pattern with added pattern forever.

This is a universe of waves *within* waves and waves *without* waves; pulsing waves of dual light, extending forever outward to the ends of mirrored space and reflecting back again to microscopic centers of rest from which they may *again* spring from rest to seek rest through dual motion, but never finding it.

This is a sex divided, opposed, two-way electric universe which creates and voids through unbalanced pairs but repeats (reproduces) through voided ones.

SEXES DO NOT UNITE

Reproduction of dynamic sexed pairs does not come through the *union* of dynamic sexed pairs, but from the *voidance of sex condition,* and with it, the power of dynamic sex expression reproduction.

Reproduction is not the unity of two opposite halves of one patterned thing; it is the voiding of the power of dynamic expression which all unbalanced opposites express.

Reproduction is the cessation of those two unbalanced conditions which restores a balance from which similarly patterned negative forms reverse their expressions and become positive forms.

SEX OPPOSITES REPRODUCE THROUGH SEX VOIDANCE

In this manner all patterned forms repeat their patterns sequentially.

All pairs of unbalanced opposites come from God, the One, and return balanced as one, to God.

All unbalanced pairs of separately conditioned things must first find voidance of unbalance and voidance of opposition. *They must then become their own opposites to again acquire an unbalance necessary for another voidance and consequent repetition.* All twos must become voided in the One in order to again become two. Reproduction of unbalanced opposites, by unbalanced opposites, is impossible. Opposition must first be voided. *The dynamic must emerge from rest and it must be voided in rest in order that it may again become dynamic.*

THE DESIRE FOR BALANCE

All things seek balance. Two opposed, unbalanced halves of one are forever seeking to balance their opposition. Two children on a seesaw are balanced when they are on a level with their centering fulcrum. When they are on two different levels they are then unbalanced with their centering fulcrum. They are then dynamic. The fulcrum no longer centers them although they are balanced in themselves. In such a position they are obliged to move. Repetition of their motion is impossible while they are in balance with their fulcrum, but is imperative when the fulcrum no longer centers them.

A sexless condition is imperative before a sexed condition can be repeated. Just as all motion starts from rest and returns to rest, so does a sexed electric condition arise from a sexless one.

The two sexes, therefore, cannot be united to cause reproduction. They must first be voided.

Unbalanced condition and change cannot *unite* to reproduce unbalanced condition and change. The unbalanced condition and change must be voided in order to repeat unbalance and change.

SEX OPPOSITES DO NOT NEUTRALIZE—THEY VOID

The sexes like the two opposites of motion cannot "neutralize" each other by so-called "union."

The dynamic cannot be "neutralized."

Likewise, it cannot *become* static. But it can be voided. The static condition does not *then* take its place, for the static condition is eternal. It was there before the dynamic condition arose.

The dynamic condition of sound, for example, arises from the static condition of silence, but sound does not *become* silence. Sound is *voided*; silence is eternal.

The dynamic conditions of sodium and chlorine do not unite to become the static condition of sodium chloride, nor are they neutralized. They must be voided before they can be repeated.

SEX DETERMINED BY DIRECTION OF PRESSURES

Opposites are not *things*; they are *conditions* of things. Just as heat and cold, or east and west, or inward and outward, or compression and expansion cannot *unite* to become one, so also, the opposite sexes cannot unite for they are but inward-outward *pressures.*

Sex opposition is a difference in the pressure *condition* of things. The male condition is one of compression, the female is one of expansion. The sexes are thus differently conditioned by the two directions of electric pressures, in accord with the two opposite desires of the Creator. The difference of conditioning makes basically similar substances appear to be different things and different substances.

All things are sex divided. When, therefore, any two opposed and unbalanced sex halves of one conditioned thing balance their opposed conditioning through motion, they appear to become another thing or substance.

This appearance is a deception of the senses for they do not become another thing. They become voided and another thing from which both are extended, appears in their place. In chemistry we call these pairs stable compounds such as the salts.

Water, for another example, is a voidance of oxygen and hydrogen, for there is no oxygen or hydrogen in water. Nor do oxygen and hydrogen *become* water. Water is the result of the voidance of two unbalanced and opposed conditions caused by equalizing opposed pressures at static equators.

Consider the static condition of the calm ocean. A storm transforms that surface into a dynamic condition.

Waves which spring from the static ocean surface toward crests and troughs do not *unite* to reproduce another wave; they *withdraw* into the ocean surface. They disappear entirely and then reappear from it in reverse to repeat the next wave.

Absolute *voidance* of one condition must take place before repetition can follow.

Voided motion is recorded in the stillness from which it was unfolded in order that it can be repeated from that record.

Records of motion are seeds for repetition of motion. In the seed is desire for manifesting imaged forms of idea. All forms are wave forms. All wave forms unfold from seed records of those wave forms.

"I am dual thinking Mind, thinking two in action and reaction.

"I am dynamic thinking Mind, pulsing with My dynamic thinking.

"With one pulsebeat of My dual thinking I build My multiple one image and bind them all as One in Me. I then cancel them with the other voiding pulse. Each then is naught, but both are seed for another two.

"Thus I produce, void and reproduce; generate, radiate and regenerate in cycles without end.

"For behold, My imaged universe is mir-

"Thus I produce, void and reproduce; generate, radiate and regenerate in cycles without end.

"For behold, My imaged universe is mirrored to infinity; it is repeated to the endless end; yet there are but multiples of three in all My universe. And again I say to thee, two of those very three are naught but My imaginings, for My Trinity is but One.

"The two are in Me, and they are of Me, but they are not Me, nor am I them."

—*From* THE DIVINE ILIAD

Chapter VIII

ELECTRICITY DEFINED

Electricity is the strain or tension set up by the two opposing desires of universal Mind thinking: the desire for balanced action and the desire for rest.

This electric universe is a complexity of strains caused by the interaction of these two opposing, interchanging electric desires.

All matter is electric. All matter is conditioned into greater or lesser strains according to the intensity of desire which is the cause of all electric strain to which it

electric desires.

All matter is electric. All matter is conditioned into greater or lesser strains according to the intensity of desire which is the cause of all electric strain to which it is subjected.

The farther removed from rest, the greater the strain or tension. That which we call high electric potential is merely great strain to maintain a condition which is far from the condition of rest.

The familiar return ball with which a child plays is a good example of electric strain. When the ball is thrown from the hand, the elastic gradually tightens to increase the tension of resistance to strain generated in the elastic. The strain continues to intensify until the ball comes to rest. When the ball returns, the strain gradually lessens until the ball again comes to rest in the child's hand. When that happens, the strain and tension have been voided. Tension has not BECOME rest; it has ceased to be.

This whole electric universe is a complex maze of similar tensions. Every particle of matter in the universe is separated from its condition of oneness, just as the return ball is separated from the hand, and each is connected with the other one by an electric thread of light which measures the tension of that separateness.

It is as though all of the universe of separated particles were playing return ball with each other. When a condition of oneness has been attained in matter, the electric tension ceases to be. Sodium chloride will illustrate this meaning. When sodium and chlorine desire separateness from their oneness of condition in sodium chloride, an electric strain is set up between that separated trinity. When the desire for separateness has gone out of sodium and chlorine, the electric tensions which bound them to the rest condition from which they sprang are voided. Likewise sodium and chlorine are utterly voided.

The reason for this is because all matter is a series of electric tensions. When the tensions cease, the conditions set up by them cease. It is as though two children on a seesaw withdrew into their fulcrum.

Sex tensions and strains intensify the farther they are removed from rest. When unbalanced sex tensions void their unbalance through interchange between the opposite electric desires which caused those tensions, electrical force ceases to be. Likewise sex desire ceases to be.

Electrical tensions exist only between unbalanced electrical matter in motion which is separated from other electrical matter in motion. Wherever there is a condition of rest, electricity ceases to be. Electricity is, therefore, a dual force which seemingly unbalances a condition of rest by dividing it into two opposite conditions and sets them in seeming motion. Interchange between the two opposites of motion voids the unbalanced condition at the end of each cycle of electric expression.

As rest cannot be unbalanced save by illusion, electricity which causes that illusion has no existence.

"Behold in Me the One, inseparable.

"Two things there are not in My universe. There is but Me.

"Everything that is is of every other thing that is. Nothing is of itself alone. All things are indissolubly united.

"This is a universe of seeming; an imaged universe of thinking; an action universe of desiring. That which Mind desireth will appear in the image of that desiring.

"This is a universe of seeming; an imaged universe of thinking; an action universe of desiring. That which Mind desireth will appear in the image of that desire.

"Seek ye, therefore, what ye will in Me and ye shall find it. Desire what ye will and behold it standeth before Thee. Throughout the aeons it hath been thine without thy knowing, e'en though thou hast but just asked for it.

"Sit ye not and ask, acting not, for thy desire will not come thy way to thee unaided by thy strong arms.

"Behold, I am within all things centering them; and I am without all things controlling them, but I am not those things which I center in them and control in space surrounding them.

"I am the center of My universe of Me. Everywhere I am is the center of all things, and I am everywhere."

—*From* THE DIVINE ILIAD

Chapter IX

THE TWO ELECTRIC DESIRES

Electricity is the servant of Mind. It does all of the work of creating this light-wave universe in unfolding-refolding sequences which Mind desires. The universal Mind has two desires—the desire for creative expression through the action of concentrative thinking and the desire for rest from action through decentrative thinking.

One desire is for separation from Oneness into unbalanced multiplicity and the other is for voidance of multiplicity into balanced Oneness. One desire is for action and the other for rest.

These two desires of Mind constitute the give for regiving principle by means of which all things in Nature grow or unfold by appearing from the void of rest in the kingdom of heaven from which all creating things appear, disappear and reappear in sequential cycles.

The electric expression of the two desires is reflected in the pulse beat of the universe. One pulsation compresses, the other expands. The compressive pulsation gives form to idea by seeking rest at wave amplitudes through centripetal action. The destructive pulsation voids form to seek rest at wave axes through centrifugal reaction.

These two opposite desires are characteristic of all effects of motion. All animal, vegetable and mineral life seeks action and rest alternately.

All effects of motion manifest that principle. A ball thrown in the air seeks rest from its action and returns from its unbalanced condition to seek rest through reaction.

After a day of work man rests from action so that he may repeat his day of action.

Because of these two opposite desires of universal Mind-thinking, all creating things appear on earths from the void of their heaven, disappear from their earths into their void in the heavens and reappear from that void to repeat their desires.

This explains the mystery of *"matter appearing from space to be alternately swallowed by space."*

"Again I say, I am the Soul of My universe of creating things.

"Within My Being is desire for manifesting My Being. Desire in Me is Soul in Me.

"That which is Soul in Me desireth to manifest in form through Light. Light extendeth from Soul in Me and returneth to Soul in Me, the extension and returning being two seeming lights of Me.

"Again I say, I am the seed of My unfolding-refolding universe. Within My Light all formless seed of planned idea are enfolded in My Being at rest in Me.

"Again I say, all things extendeth from Me and returneth to Me. From Me all things are born from seed of thought in Me, and born again, with each pulsation of My thinking.

"There is naught but birth in My imagining. There is no death in Me, for endings and beginnings are one in Me. Naught but life reacheth out from Me, and naught but life meets returning life for rebirth in Me.

"Wherefore I say, Ye must be born again and again unto that infinity of mirrored reachings which is My imagining. Thus is My One Idea continued endlessly in imaged forms of My thinking. Thus is My One Idea reborn as many ones in the multiplying mirrors of My Light, forever without end.

"Again I say, the mirrored multiples of My thought images are but reflections of My imaginings. They are not Me."

—*From* THE DIVINE ILIAD

Chapter X

THE UNFOLDING-REFOLDING PRINCIPLE

The two opposite electric expressions of desire of Mind unfold all idea of Mind from its pattern in the seed into imaged forms to simulate the idea of Mind and refold it back into its recorded pattern in the seed, for again unfolding.

Each one unbalances the other in order that each may seek balance in the other to disappear and reappear as the other.

Positive electricity is the father-light, which gravitates toward a point of rest which centers all creating things.

Negative electricity is the mother-light which radiates toward planes of the One Light at rest which bound all wave fields of motion.

Positive electricity winds the light of motion into dense solids around points of still magnetic Light. It compresses motion into incandescent spheres surrounded by the vacuity of negative electricity.

Negative electricity unwinds the light of motion from dense solidity to tenuous vacuity by expanding it into cubic wave fields of space.

Positive electricity pulls inward spirally from within

against the opposing resistance of negative electricity which thrusts *outward* spirally from within.[2]

This two-way radial universe of seeming motion is the product of these two opposed electric conditioners of matter which pass through each other in opposite directions. Each interchanges with the other in sequential pulsations as they pass through each other from points of gravity to wave field boundaries and back again in endless cycles. Each becomes the other at halfway rest points of their cycles.

Large scale examples of this process can be seen in any of the spiral nebulae, notably Nebula 74 Piscium. Two fiery spiral arms of radiating mother-light reach out from the equator of its central sun to born its countless other suns and earths by unfolding them from its centering seed. (Figs. 35 and 37, pg. 242)

Two black arms of gravitating father-light pull spirally inward from the heavens toward the poles of the centering giant sun to generate the sun in incandescent oneness of all form.[2] The father-light of gravity refolds all unfolding forms from Creation's seed in formless light of suns and gives them growing bodies.

Gravitation is the male principle of Creation. Gravity refolds toward the seed.

Radiation is the female principle of Creation. Radiation unfolds from the seed.

The generating light of gravitation and the degenerative light of radiation are projected through each other from rest to rest in pulsing sequences to manifest idea by borning father-mother forms of idea through their voiding interchange. *This principle of rhythmic balanced interchange between father-mother lights of gravitation and radiation is fundamental in all creating things.*

It is the principle of two-way equal giving which manifests the quality of Love in the Light of the One.

"Translate thou the Light of My thinking into man's words for his guidance.

"I am Balance. In Me all My imaginings are balanced in their seeming unbalance.

"I add; but that which I add to one pulsation of My thinking I subtract from the other one.

"I divide; but that which I divide I multiply.

one.

"I divide; but that which I divide I multiply.

"My pairs of opposites are equal; but again I say that they are opposites, and opposites oppose in my universe of Me.

"Opposites void opposites, while likes retain their friendly orbits side by side. All the suns of heaven give light of each to each, while the dark voids the light and the light, likewise, the dark.

"My two lights move in opposed ways to avoid the other's path, but find these paths to be lanes leading into and out of vortices centered by but one rest pole where the two poles are naught, having never even met as two.

"Pairs of opposites are drawn into each other's vortices where they void each other, passionately. Each is then naught, a zero simulating that Zero of their Source from which they sprang—but they are also seed for another seeming two which emerge from the Oneness of their Source."

—*From* THE DIVINE ILIAD

Chapter XI

THE ILLUSION OF ATTRACTION AND REPULSION OF MATTER

One of the great illusions of the senses is that matter attracts and repels matter. It is also believed that oppositely charged electrical particles attract each other and like charges repel.

There is much evidence of the senses to justify such a conclusion, but it is of the same illusive nature as the evidence which deceives the senses that railroad tracks seem to meet upon the horizon.

We see the tides rise toward the moon on one side of the earth and away from it on the other. We conclude that the moon attracts the earth and thus pulls the ocean toward it, but that does not account for the fact that the tides also rise on the opposite side of the earth away from the moon. *What is actually happening is that all conditioned matter is constantly seeking to balance its condition with all other matter.*

The moon and the earth center their own respective wave fields surrounded by space. All wave fields are bound by planes of zero curvature, and a zero pressure condition, which insulate each field in the universe from every other field. The very shapes of wave fields of earth and moon are forever changing to adjust their balance as the moon revolves around the earth. As a result, the mutual equators of both fields must lengthen, disc-like, on a plane which intersects the center of gravity of each body. Naturally the tides rise toward, and *away,* from the moon. If the earth were all liquid instead of solid, it, likewise, would lengthen appreciably at its equators, disc-like, and flatten at its poles to meet the interchange of balance between the fields of the moon and sun, as Jupiter and the outer planets are so noticeably doing. It would also throw off rings as Saturn and all the stars of heaven are doing, and for the same reason.

POLARITY

We see the positive pole of a compass needle pointing toward the negative pole of a magnet and the negative pole of the magnet pointing toward the positive pole. This evidence is one of the bases of our conclusion. That is what our eyes see. *What actually is happening is that they are voiding each other's unbalanced condition to seek balance through each other.*

Opposite poles get as far away from each other as they can, until their opposition is voided by balance in their fulcrum and they cease to be.

When the positive pole of a magnet is brought into contact with the negative pole of another magnet, that effect which we think of as attraction is one of *voidance*. It is a cessation of opposition or power to manifest anything. Polarity utterly ceases at that point and each opposite extends to each opposite end, each getting away from the other and *through* the other, spirally, as far as it can.

If opposite poles attracted each other, they would be together in the middle of a magnet instead of at its ends.

MATTER IS POWERLESS TO ATTRACT

Matter neither attracts nor repels other matter. *Unbalanced conditions in matter seek balanced ones. All matter is motion constantly seeking rest.*

This it can find only by balancing its condition with matter similarly conditioned by voiding the tensions of its sexed condition. That alone is the cause of motion and the reason for its continuance or discontinuance.

ALL MATTER IN MOTION SEEKS REST

This is a universe of ONE THING. All matter which is electrically separated from that oneness seeks it. This is a fundamental principle and underlying desire of all Creation. It is as true of humans and their emotions as it is of matter.

We again repeat that electricity is a division of the One Light into two extensions of that Light *projected through each other,* each becoming the other alternately. The One Light is a pressureless and sexless condition. The two lights which are extended from the one are opposed pressures and opposed sexed conditions.

Thus there are but two conditions of matter—either expanding from stillness or contracting toward stillness. Each condition arises from the other. The instant it becomes its own opposite it gets as far away from that opposite as is necessary to find balance in a like condition. It seeks its like condition to find rest in a balanced condition and not because the matter of it is attracted by the matter it seeks. A log floating down stream is seeking a balanced condition and is not being attracted by the dam or by other logs.

These opposites represent the compression-extension father-mother principle which integrates light into solids and disintegrates it into vapors and gases.

ALL MOVING MASSES ARE UNBALANCED

To say that these opposites attract each other is equivalent to saying that north attracts south, that inward attracts outward, that wetness attracts dryness, or that darkness attracts incandescence.

Water, for example, is a compressed condition.

When water vaporizes it expands into its own opposite condition. It then seeks rest in clouds of like condition. When it thus finds rest in a balanced condition, its motion ceases and its opposition also ceases.

ILLUSIVE EVIDENCE

Another effect of motion which has misled the senses into believing that opposites attract is that hot air is said to rise toward cold and cold air to descend toward heat. That is not what is happening, for like seeks like. *Cooling air is expanding and rising toward cold, and heating air is contracting and falling toward heat.*

Negative oxygen bubbles gather at the positive pole of a charging electric battery and positive hydrogen bubbles gather at the negative pole. What is actually happening is that the positive pole is taking the positive condition out of the water, leaving the negative oxygen as residue. The negative pole is, likewise, taking the negative condition out of the water, leaving the positive hydrogen as residue. Again like seeks like.

The outstanding demonstration of the principle of like conditions seeking like is in the elements of matter. If opposites attracted opposites according to present concepts, it would be impossible to gather together one ounce of the same elements. All elements seek their kind. In any chemical decomposition of compounded mixtures, each element seeks and finds similarly conditioned elements.

Nature's gyroscopic principle does this automatically. Every element has its own gyroscopic relation to the axis and amplitude of its wave. Each seeks that relation of pressure and moves until it finds itself in the orbit of its own gyroscopic plane of pressure.

"Behold in Me the Light of all knowing. In Light is all Idea of knowing.

"In divided Light of Me the thinking of My knowing is recorded in moving imaged forms of My imagining which reflect each divided one into its opposed one to manifest My knowing. Each mirrors light of each to the other one to manifest My knowing through their mirrorings.

"Know thou that moving things move not. Their moving is but seeming.

"Know thou also that moving things alone sense moving things and know them not, for moving things have naught in them but their seeming moving.

"Moving light of My thinking's mirrorings is My universe of image building in lights of My imaginings. These have no Being, for they are not Me. I alone have Being."

—*From* THE DIVINE ILIAD

Chapter XII

LIGHT

Light cannot be seen; it can only be known. Light is still. The sense of sight cannot respond to stillness. That which the eyes "feel" and believe to be Light is but wave motion simulating the idea of Light. Like all things else in this electric wave universe the idea of Light cannot be produced. Electric waves simulate idea only. They do not *become* idea.

When man sees the light of the sun he believes that he is actually seeing light when the nerves of his eyes are but "feeling" the intense, rapid, shortwave vibrations of the kind of wave motion which he senses as incandescence. The intensely vibrant electric current mirrored into the senses of the eyes fairly burns them. They cannot stand that high rate of vibration. The eyes would be destroyed by such a vibration, but light would not be the cause of that destruction. Fast motion, simulating light, would be the cause. It would be like sending a high voltage electric current over a wire so fine that the current would burn it out.

Man likewise cannot see darkness. The nerves of his eyes which sense motion slow down to a rate of vibration which he can no longer "feel."

Man is so accustomed to the idea that he actually sees light in various intensities illuminating various substances to greater or lesser degree that it is difficult for him to realize that his own senses are but acting as mirrors to reflect various intensities of wave motion. But that is all that is happening.

Every electrically conditioned thing in Nature reflects the vibrations of every other thing, to fulfill its desire to synchronize its vibrations with every other thing. All matter is the motion of light. All motion is expressed in waves. All light waves are mirrors which reflect each other's condition unto the farthermost star.

This is an electrically conditioned wave universe. All wave conditions are forever seeking oneness. For this reason all sensation responds to all other sensation.

IS LIGHT A WAVE OR CORPUSCLE?

Much controversy has arisen as to whether light is corpuscular, as Newton claimed it to be, or a wave. There is much evidence in favor of both theories. It is both. Light is expressed by motion. All motion is wave motion. All waves are expressed by fields of equal and opposite pressures of two-way motion. The entire volume within wave fields is filled with the two opposite expressions of motion—the positive expression which compresses light into solids, and the negative expression which expands it into space surrounding solids.

All space within wave fields is curved. Curvature ends at planes of zero curvature which bound all wave fields. These boundary planes of omnipresent magnetic Light act as mirrors to reflect all curvature into all other wave fields in the universe, and as fulcrums from which motion in one wave field is universally repeated.

ALL MATTER IS WAVE MOTION

Together these constitute what we call matter and space. It has been difficult to conceive light as being purely corpuscular, for light is presumed to fill all space. Space is not empty. It is full of wave motion. Corpuscles of matter are one half of wave cycles of light. Space is the other half.

There need be no mystery as to whether light is corpuscular or wave, for waves of motion which simulate the light and darkness of space are all there is.

The light and motion of solid matter, and of gaseous matter of space, differs only in volume and condition. Water of earth is compressed into small volume while water of the heavens is expanded thousands of time in volume. Each condition is the opposite half of the cycle of water.

Water vapor is water turned inside-out. It again

becomes water by turning outside-in. Expansion-contraction sequences result from this process.

ALL MATTER IS SIMULATED LIGHT

Water of the heavens still is water, and it still is light waves. No change whatsoever has taken place between the waters of earth and those of the heavens except a change of its condition from positive to negative preponderance. This change is due solely to a change of its direction in respect to its center of gravity.

All dense cold matter, such as iron, stone, wood, and all growing or decaying things, are light. We do not think of them as light but all are waves of motion, and all waves of motion are light.

Light is all there is in the *spiritual* universe of knowing, and *simulation* of that Light in opposite extensions is all there is in the electric wave universe of sensing. The simulation of Light in matter is not Light. There is no Light in matter.

Perhaps the confusion which attends this idea would be lessened if we classify everything concerning the spiritual universe, such as life, intelligence, truth, power, knowledge and balance as being the ONE LIGHT of KNOWING, and everything concerning matter and motion as being the TWO SIMULATED LIGHTS of thinking.

Thinking expresses knowing in matter but matter does not think, nor does it know.

Thinking also expresses life, truth, idea, power and balance by recording the ideas of those qualities in the two lights of matter in motion, but matter does not live, nor is it truth, balance or idea, even though it *simulates* those spiritual qualities.

Man's confusion concerning this differentiation lies in his long assumption of the reality of matter. His assumption that his body is his Self, that his knowledge is in his brain, and that he lives and dies because his body integrates and disintegrates, has been so fundamental a part of his thinking that it is difficult for him to reverse his thinking to the fact that matter is but motion and has no reality beyond simulating reality.

The light which we think we see is but motion. We do not *see* light. We *feel* the wave vibrations set up by the motion which simulates light, but the motion of electric waves which simulate light is not that which it simulates.

CONFUSION CONCERNING LIGHT CORPUSCLES

There is much confusion concerning the many kinds of particles of matter such as electrons, protons, photons, neutrons and others. These many particles are supposedly different because of the belief that some are negatively charged, some are positively charged and some are so equally charged that one supposedly neutralizes the other.

There is no such condition in nature as negative charge, nor are there negatively charged particles. Charge and discharge are opposite conditions, as filling and emptying, or compressing and expanding are opposite conditions.

Compressing bodies are charging into higher potential conditions. Conversely, expanding bodies are discharging into lower potential conditions. To describe an electron as a negatively charged body is equivalent to saying that it is an expanding-contracting body.

Contracting and expanding bodies move in opposite directions. Contracting bodies move radially inward toward mass centers, and expanding bodies move radially outward toward space which surrounds masses. In this two-way universe, light which is inwardly directed toward gravity charges mass and discharges space. When directed toward space it charges space and discharges mass. All direction of force in Nature is spiral.

The charging condition is positive. It multiplies speed of motion into density of substance. The principle of multiplication of motion because of decrease of volume is the cause of the acceleration of gravity. The discharging condition is negative. It divides speed of motion into tenuity of substance. The principle of the division of motion because of expansion of volume, is the cause of the deceleration of radiation.

One can better comprehend this principle by knowing that what we call substance is purely motion. Motion simulates substance by its variation of pressures, its speed and its gyroscopic relation to its wave axis.

Particles are variously conditioned as to pressure but there are no different kinds of particles. All are light waves wound up into particles which are doubly charged. Their position at any one point in their wave causes them to have the electric condition appropriate for that point.

Light particles are forever moving in their octave waves. All are either heading toward their cathode or their anode, which means toward vacuity or gravity. They are all moving either inward or outward, spirally.

ALL LIGHT PARTICLES ARE ALIKE

All light particles are either expressing the mother-light principle or the father-light principle. For example, if a particle is on the amplitude of the wave, it would be a true sphere, and as a true sphere it would be neither positive nor negative. It might then appropriately be called a neutron. A particle which is spirally heading inward toward the apex of a vortex in the process of becoming a sphere might appropriately be called a proton, because of its expressing the father-light principle.

Again, if it is moving spirally outward, it could appropriately be called an electron because it would then be discharging in excess of its charge or expanding in excess of its contraction.

Light rays, for example, leaving the sun, are discharging the sun. They are also discharging themselves because they are expanding into greater volume. They are also lowering their own potential by multiplying their volume. They reverse their polarity when radially converging upon the earth. They are then charging the earth and themselves by contracting into smaller volume and are simultaneously multiplying their own potential by thus contracting.

SEMI-CYCLIC ALTERATION

In an electric current there is a constant interchange between anode and cathode or positive and negative poles. A light particle expands as it leaves the anode in an outward radial direction and contracts as it radially approaches the anode.[3] This light particle has been the same light particle at all times in all parts of its journey. Its variation of charge and discharge, its direction of motion and the condition of wave pressure in which it finds itself at any time are the sole reasons for its changing from one condition to another. The light particles are all the same light particles, all being different only in pressure condition.

This is also true of the elements of matter. Whether they be iron, carbon, silicon, bismuth or radium, all are composed of the same kind of light particles.

They all seem to have different qualities and attributes, but those qualities and attributes are likewise given to them purely by the positions they occupy in their waves.

ALL THINGS SIMULATE LIGHT

A particle of light which belongs to an atomic system of sodium has in it all of the entire range of the elements, besides all of every other creating thing in the universe. It acts to carry out the purposefulness of the idea of sodium simply because it is in the pressure condition of sodium, and is a part of the unfolding pattern of the seed of inert gas of the octave from which it has unfolded.

If that same particle unfolded from the seed of the oak, it would be part of the wood fiber of its trunk, or leaf, or of the chlorophyll which colored its leaves, but it would be the same kind of particle while fulfilling the purpose of cellulose as while fulfilling the purpose of sodium.

All matter in this universe is but differently conditioned motion simulating light, and all differences in condition are pressure differences.

LIGHT DOES NOT TRAVEL

The speed with which light presumably travels is 186,400 miles per second. The distance between stars is so great that the speed of light is computed as light years, for the distance computed by lesser units of time would yield figures so great that they would be meaningless.

Light only seems to travel. It is but one more of the countless illusions caused by wave motion. Waves of the ocean seem to traverse the ocean but they only appear to do so, for waves are pistons in the universal engines, and pistons operate up and down. Wave pistons of light, or of the ocean, operate radially and spirally inward and outward, toward and away from gravity.

Waves of light do not travel. They reproduce each other from wave field to wave field of space. The planes of zero curvature which bound all wave fields act as mirrors to reflect light from one field into another. This sets up an appearance of light as travelling, which is pure illusion.

The sunlight we feel upon our bodies is not actual light from the sun. What actually is happening is that the sun is reproducing its own condition on the earth by extending the reproductions out through cold space into ever enlarging wave fields until those reproductions begin to converge again toward our center of gravity into ever smaller wave fields. The heat we feel and the light we see are dependent entirely upon the ability of the wave fields to reproduce the light and heat, and that ability is conditioned upon the amount of moisture in the atmosphere.

If there were no moisture in the atmosphere, our bodies would carbonize from the heat thus reproduced. One cannot consistently think of that heat as direct rays of the sun, for that same sunlight was intensely cold during its reproduced journey through the immensely expanded wave fields of space between the sun and earth.

The light and heat which appear to come from the star or sun have never left the star or sun.

That which man sees as light and feels as heat are the reproduced counterparts of the light and heat which are its cause.

The rate of vibration in a wave field depends upon its volume. Vibration in a wave field means the pulse of interchange between its compressed core and the space surrounding that core. A slow vibration in a large wave field would cool one's body, or even freeze it, while fast pulsing interchange in extremely small wave fields could burn one's body.

A lens which multiplies light and heat toward a focal point which sets paper on fire merely compresses larger wave fields into smaller ones. The rate of vibration increases for the same reason that the planets nearest the sun move much faster in their small orbits than those which are far away from the sun. Kepler's law covering the speeds of planets will apply to rates of vibration in wave fields as appropriately as with the movements in the solar system.

"The imaged universe of My dual thinking is a two-way interchanging between unbalanced lever ends of light which extend from Me, their fulcrum of power in Rest, and return to Me.

"Behold in Me the fulcrum of My changing universe which manifests change, though I change not, nor move.

"For I am Rest. In Me alone is Balance.

"He who would find power must know that he extends from Me, that I am he.

"He who would find rest must return to Me, be Me, be fulcrum of his own power."

—*From* THE DIVINE ILIAD

Chapter XIII

CYCLES

All energy is expressed in wave cycles.

A cycle is a two-way electric journey from a compression point of rest where gravity ceases and radiation begins, to an expansion point of rest at wave field boundaries where radiation ceases and gravity begins. It is the universal heartbeat of this pulsing universe of two-way motion.

The life-death cycle of man is one wave in an electric current. Growth and decay, or the incoming-outgoing breath, are two halves of cycles.

Matter is expressed in two-way cycles because matter is but a record of God's knowing, expressed by the two opposed desires of His two-way self-voiding thinking.

All Nature is an expression of the two desires of the Creator, the desire for separation from the oneness of rest in Him into a multiplicity of imaged forms of His imagining, and for a voidance of that multiplicity by a return to rest in His oneness.

A cycle is like winding and unwinding a clock spring except that matter is wound up into visible spheres and unwound into invisible cubes. The unwinding of a clock spring is a reverse process from that of its winding. Nature is continuous. It never reverses, like the piston in an engine, or two children on a seesaw.

Nature turns its waves inside-out and outside-in in a continuous spiral flow of direction. Solid matter gradually interchanges with space in its breathing cycles until gravitation has attained its maximum. Radiation then exceeds the power of gravitation and matter begins to expand instead of to contract.

Radiation is light outwardly bound from the seed. Gravitation is light inwardly bound toward the seed. Outwardly bound light manifests the unfolding of patterned light from the seed. It is the mother of Creation. Inwardly bound light manifests the refolding of patterned light into its seed. It is the father of Creation.

The mother of Creation gives patterned bodies to idea by unfolding idea unto the heavens. That is the first half of every cycle. The father refolds all unfolding idea back toward its seed, otherwise the unfolding form could not become visible as matter. That is the second half of every cycle. All growing things manifest this unfolding and refolding process in every pulsation of interchange between the father-mother lights of Creation.

The outward-inward breath of all things is the constant interchanging cyclic process by means of which one opposite gradually becomes the other until each becomes the other in totality by completing the interchange.

Each outward-inward breath is a cycle. Each half-cycle is cancelled by its other half until both are cancelled. Neither then manifests. Both disappear into their equilibrium to reappear as the other.

Life and death gradually interchange to cancel each other for the purpose of repeating the cycle of life and death.

Death is born in the same cradle with life, but life is strong while death is weak. From the very first breath of the newborn babe, death voids life by each outward breath and life voids death by each inward breath. At maturity, death has become balanced with life and death then becomes stronger until both disappear to reappear with life as the stronger and death the weaker opposite.

THIS EXPANDING UNIVERSE

It is said that the universe is expanding to a heat death, that all heat is gradually going out of the universe, leaving it utterly cold and empty.

It is believed that radiation is a "downhill flow of energy" which is not compensated for by an equal "uphill flow." Radiation is known as radiant energy.

Radiation is but the outbreathing of this universal body which breathes in its entirety exactly as man and all things else in Nature breathe. Radiation is the unfolding mother-light.

The inbreathing of Nature is gravitation. Gravitation is the father-light which refolds that which unfolds.

For every drop of water that "radiant energy" discharges from the earth, "gravitation energy" charges it with falling waters. One of these opposites is the downhill flow of expressed energy and the other is its equal uphill flow.

Every creating thing in this universe has a father and a mother, not only animal and vegetable life but every corpuscle of matter in the universe. Likewise every creating thing is both father and mother. The mother borns the father and the father borns the mother. The proton borns the electron and the electron the proton. Each was the other and each sequentially becomes the other through the pulsing breath of wave interchange.

DECEPTIVE EVIDENCE

One of the illusions which deceived man into believing that God's universal body was dying was the discovery that all nebulae are rushing away from each other with incredible velocities. This fact would lead to the utter dissolution of the universe in time. The so-called "red shift" in the spectrum proved this to be fact.

The fact is true. They do rush away from each other, but the conclusion drawn from that observed fact is not justified by the processes of natural law. The reason for the universal expansion which is now taking place is that the universe as a whole breathes inward and outward just as all things in nature do.

Large-scale breathing cycles of the whole universal body consume untold aeons for the completion of one cycle while man consumes but a few seconds to complete his cycle. Man of aeons to come will witness the effect of nebulae rushing toward each other at the same speeds for the same number of aeons.

In all Nature there is no effect of motion which is not balanced by an opposite effect. The universe is sexed throughout. One sex cannot exist without the other. "Radiant energy" is impossible without generative energy to born it.

The desire of the Creator for separateness must be balanced with His desire for oneness. The expansion stroke of the universal piston must have a balancing compression stroke in order that the universal body may manifest the life of its Creator.

The whole universe slowly expands toward the death half of its breathing cycle, and then contracts toward the life half of it.

Every separate mass in the universe is in its own part of its cycle, either inbreathing toward the high point of its maturity or outbreathing toward its resurrection. Each one, whether generating or degenerating, is being generated into extended life by the inbreathing of the whole, of which each is an indissoluble part.

"In My imaged universe all things are two, centered by Me, for all things extend from the dual, two-way moving pendulum of My thinking, and My thinking is two. I, the One Light, center the two lights which register My thinking, but I am not those two lights, nor am I My thinking.

"Behold in Me the Trinity, the One extended unto the two, the One Creator centering the extended two.

"In My imaged universe all effect is also two: all thermal measures and the weights of things; the two of matter, and of time, and direction; the two of color, and of the elements; the two of the wave of My thinking, and its expressions. The very One Light of Me is extended in the two lights of My imagining.

"Naught is there in all My universe which is not part and counterpart pairs of things, equal and opposite counterpart pairs of creating and repeating things, each seeking to unbalance each, and each forever seeking balance in each.

"For behold, I am Light, but the universe of My imagining is dual light; light divided and multiplied by common root directly and inversely applied to all things which forever move two ways between the two extended lights of their centering One to express My knowing by My thinking."

—*From* THE DIVINE ILIAD

Chapter XIV

WEIGHT

Weight is a measure of unbalance. It indicates the intensity of desire of any mass which is out of balance to find balance.

Every mass in the universe has its proper potential position. Every mass will find that position if not prevented from doing so by the bindings of other masses.

Weight should be measured dually as temperature is. It should have an above and a below zero to measure the intensity of desire in masses to rise from the earth as well as to fall toward it.

WEIGHT IS MATTER OUT OF PLACE

All matter is a record of its potential at the place of its birth in its wave. Masses of matter, like buoys floating in the ocean to mark courses for ships, are floating in space to register the electric potential of the position of their birth.

Whenever matter is in the place of its birth, it belongs there. It is, therefore, in balance. It floats in its balanced field. In that position it is weightless in respect to anything else in the universe. Whenever it is taken from its field center, or becomes an eccentric part of another field, it is out of balance with the two forces acting upon it. *It then has weight, and the measure of that weight is the measure of its unbalance with its out-of-place environment.*

Weight of matter and measure of electric potential are one and the same thing.

WEIGHT IS UNBALANCE

A body which floats has no measurable weight. It is in balance with its environment. Likewise, a dead battery has no measurable electric potential. The ammeter needle points to zero. Its two unbalanced conditions of charge and discharge have become voided by each other.

The measure called "weight" and the measure called "electric potential" are the expression of force which the two electric opposites of charge and discharge exert against each other at any point in the universe.

The potential of all orbits of matter in space in which matter floats is equal to the potential of the mass which floats in it.

The plane of our earth's equatorial region coincides with an equipotential plane of pressure which is equally balanced in respect to that part of the earth which floats above that plane, and that part which floats below it. In this plane the earth has no weight whatsoever in respect to anything in the entire universe, for it is in a balanced position in respect to the entire universe and keeps moving into a new position only because of the movement of all other masses in the universe.

OUR BALANCED EARTH IS WEIGHTLESS

The earth could have weight only if removed to other pressures farther extended from the plane of the lens-like wheel of which our sun is the hub. If it could be pushed toward the sun by some giant hand, it would seek balance in its own orbit when released, exactly as a man would rise when plunged beneath his own balance level in water. Every freely moving mass in the universe floats in its own equally divided wave field exactly as a man floats in water.

The moon is not falling upon the earth, as generally supposed, for it is in balance with its environment and cannot fall. Its contracted mass is equal to the expanded mass it displaces in its wave field.

For the same reason a cloud floats in the sky. If one could put scales under it, one would find it had no weight unless lifted above or thrust below its equipotential level. If it condensed into heavier vapor, it would fall to seek a new static equator where it would again float. If it condensed to rain, it would fall into the sea to find balance in a like condition.

Weight is not a fixed property of matter. It is as variable as matter is variable.

A man weighs less as he climbs a mountain, weighs more as he descends into a mine, and weighs nothing when he floats in water.

Unless, and until, matter is extended from a plane of equal pressure, there can be no weight, nor can there be electric potential.

WEIGHT CURVES GRAVITY

The equilibrium of sea level is a good example. If that static equator has no dynamic wave extensions, there can be no electric pressures exerted to express in weight, nor could there be weight of waves when waves are not extended from it. Waves above sea level have a positive weight when they fall toward gravity. Waves below sea level have negative weight when they rise toward space to find balance at sea level.

Weight is, therefore, but a dimension of unbalance. *Unbalance alone can be weighed, for there can be no weight to balance.*

WEIGHT DEFINED

The following definitions of weight are in keeping with Natural Law.

Weight is the sum of the differences between the two pressures which act upon every mass.

Weight is the measure of the differences in electric potential between any mass and the volume it occupies.

Weight is the measure of unbalance between any mass and its displaced environment.

Weight is the measure of the force which a body exerts in seeking its true potential.

Weight is the sum of the difference between the inward pull of gravitation and the outward thrust of radiation.[2]

Weight is the measure of intensity of the desire within all matter to express motion or seek rest from motion.

"For again I say, each of the two lights which giveth form to My knowing, through My thinking, giveth its all to the other one to become the other one, sequentially.

"Light giveth to darkness to again become light, as life giveth to death to again become life. Likewise darkness of heaven giveth darkness unto suns to again become dark, as suns giveth light unto heavens to again become suns.

"Thuswise all things of earth giveth unto heavens to again become earth-things by the giving of heavens. Thus do all My creating things simulate the oneness of My knowing by interchanging their all for Oneness in Me. That interchanging records My knowing in pulsations of My thinking but My thinking is not Me. My knowing is alone Me."

—*From* THE DIVINE ILIAD

Chapter XV

THE SOURCE OF SOLAR ENERGY

One of the greatest mysteries of science is the source of the sun's renewing energy.

At the present rate of solar radiation, the sun should have burned out long ago.

What keeps its fires burning? What is it that generates heat in the sun to keep it from cooling?

One theory is that its contraction generates it, for contraction supposedly heats.

But that is not the answer, for contraction does not heat nor generate. Contraction is possible only as a *result* of generation, not as its *cause.*

Generation must precede contraction. It does not follow it.

Heat follows as a result of contraction. Heat radiates. Radiation is the opposite of generation, and opposites act in opposite ways.

Radiation expands and the resultant expansion cools; while generation contracts and the resultant contraction heats.

Here again is the father-mother principle manifesting its law of equal, opposite and sequential interchange.

The cold of expanded space generates the sun's heat by compressing large volume into smaller volume.

The high pressure of incandescence is born from the low pressure of vacuous blackness, in accordance with the law of rhythmic balanced interchange between all pairs of father-mother opposites.

THE TEMPERATURE CYCLE

The temperature cycle resulting from balanced interchange between the cold of space and the heat of suns is as follows: cold generates; generation contracts; contraction heats; heat radiates; radiation expands, and expansion cools.

Thus our hot sun is being generated from cold space via its poles and is radiated back again into space via its equator in accord with the father-mother reciprocative process of inside-out outside-in turning, and will continue to generate increasing heat in the sun until it becomes a true sphere. This spherical perfection has not yet been attained, for the sun has not yet reached the amplitude of its wave where all forming matter becomes true spheres.

ONE OPPOSITE BORNS THE OTHER

When the amplitude position is attained, its radiation will then begin to exceed its generation. It will be in the same condition as a man who has just passed his maturity high point when death and life interchange their preponderances.

From that point on, cold space will bore a black hole through the sun from pole to pole and it will expand into a giant ring centered by a smaller sun recondensed from the remnant of its expanding self. Many such ring nebulae are visible in the heavens, notably in the Lyra Ring Nebula (M. 57). (Fig. 61 pg. 252).

THE STARS TELL THE WHOLE STORY

Excellent examples of the degeneration of a sun into a ring or rings by the inside-out turning process of negative electricity are The Owl Nebula, (M. 97) in Ursae Majoris and the Dumb Bell Nebula in Vulpeculae. (Fig. 62 pg. 252).

One can likewise witness this inside-out turning process in his kitchen range. Jets of burning gas are seen as a blue and green flame around black holes which center each jet. These gases are negatively preponderant, which means that they are thrusting out from their center in excess of pulling inward from it.[2]

"He who seeketh life without the Light will find death; but he who seeketh the Light will find eternal life even when he walketh toward death.

"He who knoweth not the Light shall die to find it, but he who knoweth the Light shall never die.

"In man's inhaling there is life, and death trails his exhaling, yet must man breathe out to live again and deeply in that he may die.

"Know thou then that I alone live. I do not die, but out of Me cometh both seeming life and death.

"Life is but the inward flow of My thinking's divided pulsing, and death is its outward flow.

"Know also that the divisions of My thinking are but equal halves of One; for I again say that I am One; and that all things which come from Me are One, divided to appear as two.

"All things come and go from My divided thinking.

"All coming things are living things, and those which go are dead.

"Know thou that all creating things are resurrected from the dead, and dead things live again through My divided thinking.

"Again I say that all things are bound as One through Light.

"I am forever creating My living body and destroying it in seeming death that it may live in Me to die and live again.

"The end of life in death is life's new beginning. Both life and death are one in Me.

"All things are forever living and forever dying; and while they live they die; and also while they are in death they live.

"Such is My decree, My universal law, from which there is no escape for man, or star, or grain of sand; for all things flow from Me that they may appear to man, and return to Me, that they may disappear from his senses in the cycle of My thinking.

"I am the repetitive God. All things which

flow to Me and from Me flow again both ways through Me forever in a cycle which ends not, nor has begun.

"From My right hand life flows one way and returneth to Me full spent as death, while full death floweth the other way and returneth to Me renewed as life. Around My cycle both life and death wend their opposed ways, each seeking each until the twain meet balanced at maturity, where each gives half to each. But when they pass that halfway point on their separate ways to Me, each then gives thought to each, and then both know, as they return to Me, that each are both, and both are One in Me.

"Death is the seed of life.

"Death rebounds from death as life.

"From death life springeth from the soil; and from life death floweth even as the perfume leaves the rose.

"Death giveth of itself to life that life may live; and likewise life giveth to death that death may die.

"Life is regenerating death, and death is life degenerating.

"Light leaves thy sun as death and comes to thee as life; and when thy death leaves thee it likewise becomes new life to whom or in what its impact quickens with thy death.

"Two ways there are of breath, the inward-charging breath of life and the outward-discharging breath of death. All opposed pairs of My divided thinking pass in opposite ways along these two paths in their traversing of My cycle.

"All things which I have divided into pairs of opposites have within them both life and death; but one of these is greater than the other until they meet as equals halfway round My life-death cycle. When once they meet, and pass, they then exchange these qualities, the greater growing lesser and the lesser growing greater.

"Even though life is full when life is born, death emanates from life itself as death, and takes the opposite path toward death.

"Likewise, does life emanate from death to weaken it when death is strong, until life conquereth death to make death live as life.

"Verily I say, life cannot live without dying as it lives. Nor can death conquer life and gather aught to it but death.

"Life is My multiplying breath of compressive action; and death is My dividing, opposed breath which expands as life's reaction.

"Hear thou Me when I again say that life and death are opposites which pass each other on My cycle going opposite ways. Life attracteth life to life by its compression and death repeleth both death and life by its expansion.

"I am the interchanging point of life and death. I balance life with death; and never in their changing can either death or life outbalance death or life.

"Write thou that death and life are one, as the swinging pendulum is one, e'en though it oscillates two ways in its incessant swinging.

"He who travels East in My curved universe arrives at West as surely as he who travels West.

"Likewise life traileth the eastern road to arrive at death, while death taketh the western road where life awaiteth to quicken death as life.

"So also does death traileth the road of life to interchange with life, while life likewise traileth the road of death to find itself through death.

"Hear thou Me say there is no death in all My imagined universe. In it is naught but Life, for naught but Life and Love is in Me and My knowing.

"Naught is there in My thinking which is not My knowing; and naught but Life and Love are in My thinking.

"Take thou man's death away from him in this new day of man. Give him eternal Life in Me by knowing Me in him."

—*From* THE DIVINE ILIAD

Chapter XVI

THE LIFE PRINCIPLE

For centuries man has been searching for the life principle in germs of matter. He might as well cast his nets into the sea to search for oxygen.

There is no life in matter, nor is there death, for matter is but motion. Motion begins and ends, to begin again, but life is immortal. It has no beginning. It has no ending. It cannot die.

Man has long believed his body to be his Self, the Person, the Being. *Man's body is but motion. It can have no Being.* God dwells in man. The Person, the Being in man, is immortal. Life in him is God in him. The body of man manifests God in him by manifesting life in life-death-resurrection sequences, as all creating-decreating-recreating things in Nature likewise do.

The body of man must be forever reborn unto the endless end to manifest God in him. There is naught but birth in this cyclic, pulsing universe. There is no death.

The idea of man is a part of the One Whole Idea of Creation. All Creation is but an expression of that One Idea, part by part, each being a part of the Whole. God gives an eternal repetition of bodies to all parts of His Idea to manifest that idea in wave cycles of the divided light of His thinking. One half of each cycle unfolds the idea into the form of that idea and gives it action for producing that form. The other half of the cycle refolds the idea to give it rest in the Light of its Source for the purpose of repeating the manifestation in a repetition of that body.

A return to rest in the Light is not death; it is a return to Life for the purpose of rebirth to again manifest Life in a renewed body.

We do not say that man is dead when he rests in sleep to partially renew his body. We know that he will awaken with new parts of his body to replace those which have served their purpose and disappeared.

When man's whole body wears out and needs replacement, he likewise rests in a longer sleep. Man's body is but patterned waves of light in motion. Waves disappear into the ocean's calm but they reappear.

The ocean is a part of the idea of Creation. Waves express the idea of the power of the ocean but the power and the idea are in the calm of the ocean whether expressed by waves or not.

The turbulence of the ocean springs from its calm just as the movement of the lever springs from its still fulcrum. All motion is a two-way extension of stillness.

We do not think that the ocean is dead while it is at

rest in its calm, for we know that it will again manifest its power by waves of motion when desire is strong enough in it for manifesting it by motion.

Waves of light which give transient form to a man's body are but his body. They are not the man, nor the man-idea. The *body* of the man is an extension of other waves of father-mother light in the sun, and the *idea* of man exists in the still Light which centers the sun.

Man can never die for he is omnipresent Light and he exists everywhere. Likewise man's body cannot die for man's body manifests immortal man, and immortal man always has a body in which to manifest.

This body which extends from the earth disappears into the heavens and the earth, but that which disappears to sensed man of earth has not ceased to be, for its pattern has been recorded for repetition. It still IS and will reappear.

The senses of man are not attuned to the rest of the cycle of man's bodily journey from disappearance to reappearance but man's knowing reaches out over the entire cycle and man can know eternal repetitiveness of his body when he knows God in him.

When water disappears beyond the senses as water vapor and gases, we know they will reappear as water when they have completed their cyclic journey. As man knows the Light in him he will as surely know that he will return for aeons to complete the purpose of manifesting his Creator as one part of the Whole Idea. That purpose cannot be completed in one life cycle, nor in ten times ten million life cycles. Man has but begun to express the man-idea on this planet. He still has a long way to go, and the body he needs in which to manifest will return to him as surely as the light of day reappears from the darkness of night into which it has disappeared.

WHAT HAPPENS AFTER "DEATH"

The unanswered mystery of "where do we go when we die" needs a comprehensive answer. Abstractions and theories are not satisfying. Nature's processes are simple and are all alike. What happens to one thing which disappears happens to all things. There are no exceptions to this process of Nature.

All things in this solar system come from the sun and return to it.

The "life germ" for which man is seeking is in the sun. The idea of man is in the sun; likewise all idea of all things is in the sun awaiting birth into form. The pulsing light of polarity borns all idea into its form when conditions are favorable for each idea to be mothered by an extension of the sun.

Everything in Nature is a moving extension from a still point of the One Light. The center of the sun in our solar system is the point of still Light from which everything in the entire solar system radiates spirally, and toward which it gravitates spirally for its resurrection into another cycle.

The sun is the seed of this solar system from which all manifestations of idea in this entire system extend, and to which they return.

Motion is for the sole purpose of manifesting idea. All idea springs from a state of rest in its seed. As it unfolds from its seed, it refolds into it. It therefore follows that motion is a seeming two-way extension-retraction from and to a point and has no existence save to senses which sense but the extension, and not the voiding simultaneous retraction.

All the suns of all the heavens are centered by the still points of omnipresent Light from which all idea extends and returns. Suns are seeds of idea. From those seeds all form emerges. To those seeds all form returns.

The earth has been extended from the sun for that very purpose. Organic life is part of God's One Whole Idea. Organic life cannot be expressed in form in the sun although the idea of it is there. Everything which appears on earth as form of idea is in the sun as concept of that idea in the seed. The seed is the father-light which extends its idea of man and other creating things out into far space where its children, the planets, have sufficiently cooled to manifest the man-idea in organic form.

Suns are crucibles which born their children, the earths, and set them out to cool in order that God's idea which is in the formless suns, can manifest form in the sun's extensions.

SUNS ARE THE SEEDS OF CREATION

The Creator scatters His seeds of light throughout all space to father and mother all borning imaged forms of His imagining.

In the still center of suns is all idea for borning into the images of God's imagining, but in the oneness of the light of suns they are without form and void. All seeds are without form and void even though the pattern of all idea is in them.

The oneness of incandescent suns must be divided and extended to cooling earths before the ideas of the mineral, vegetable and animal kingdoms can sequentially unfold to prepare the way for man's unfolding from his seed in the sun.

All expression of idea of earth is likewise in the sun and must be extended to earth for manifestation. Mountains and oceans are in the sun but also all things else, the crying sound of a newborn babe, the roar of an avalanche or the street noises of a city. All of these are light, and such expressions of the Light are possible only through division and extension of the One Light into the two which manifest the One.

Millions of years ago this planet became sufficiently far from the sun for the water idea to be expressed as pairs of opposites and organic life appeared upon the earth in lowly forms. These forms gradually complexed until the man-idea began to be expressed, *not by a germ*, but by the polarization of light itself, as manifested in the interchanging heartbeat of the father-mother light of the universe.

The *idea* of all things is omnipresent in the One still Light. The *expression* of all idea is extended to the two lights of white suns and black space surrounding suns which manifest the Creator's two desires.

Desire for expression is manifested by the electric action-reaction sequences of interchange between the two opposing white and black lights of suns and space. It is this interchange which polarizes the still seed of idea into unfolding form of that idea.

To polarize means to divide stillness into opposing pulsing extensions. It is like extending a lever from a fixed fulcrum and setting it in motion to express the idea which is in the still fulcrum.

In this manner the womb of mother earth becomes impregnated with the seed of the man-idea extended from the sun, and the first cell of man unfolds from mother earth into the heavens toward the refolding light of the father.

This first pulsation of the mother-light which is borning God's idea into patterned form is the black light negative half of its pulsation cycle. The unfolding mother-light which reaches out into the heavens is the black light of expansion. Black light is the negative pattern of the positive idea of light as expressed by incandescence. In other words, black light is expanded, or unfolded, white light. Conversely, white incandescent light is contracted, or refolded black light.

This is Nature's method of giving formed bodies to formless idea. The positive father-light refolds the unfolding negative mother-light in cyclic wave pulsations which man calls "growth," but growth is but a moving picture of sequential patterns of unfolding idea projected upon the imagined three-dimensional screen of time and space.

This is the Creator's method of electrically recording His One Whole Idea in many electrically sensed multi-patterned body forms of matter.

LIFE AND DEATH OF BODIES

To understand the meaning of life and death, we must know more of Nature's processes, especially those concerning our body, and the spirit within which motivates the body and forever records our constantly changing individuality. We must know the basis of our individuality and the reason for its constant changing. In order to understand "what happens after death," we must become more fully aware of Nature's processes which give us bodies and take them away to regive new bodies to fulfill Nature's law of repetition.

Man's electrically sensed body is not the immortal man which his body manifests. His body is not the individual to which he attributes his life and Being. His body is composed of a few chemical elements borrowed from earth and sun to fashion into an instrument for his use.

When his body disappears, the individual which inhabited that body is not dead. Every body emerges from a formless state into a formed one in repeated cycles of appearance, disappearance and reappearance.

All creating things are formless as *idea* at their Source. They then unfold into *formed* idea through desire to unfold. This process of emergence from a formless state and a return to that state has been going on within man's body since its beginning.

All bodies of all creating things are forever turning inside-out and outside-in during their entire cycles. During a small part of the cycle, bodies are within the range of human sensing, but during the greater part of the cycle they are beyond that range. At no time during the entire cycle are creating things without bodies, or patterned records of bodies, from which new bodies will again spring true to their patterned records.

Each inbreathing-outbreathing cycle is unfolding the

form of a new body from an already existent patterned record. The constant refolding process which man calls death is recorded as it refolds for repetition in his next life cycle.

Nature records every action and desire of the body, likewise every conscious desire and thought of the soul in those cosmic elements which are called "the inert gases"—helium, neon, krypton, argon and others. These cosmic elements, which will not unite with the physical elements, are the basis of God's recording system by means of which every thought and action of every creating thing is stored in them as seed-extensions from sun and earth centers for repetition until their purposes are fulfilled.

Everything in Nature is purposeful and nothing in Nature fulfills its purpose in one life cycle.

Nature *multiplies the time dimensions* of her light waves so that patterned records of forms which have expanded beyond man's range of sensing can come within that range, then *divides those time dimensions* until they again disappear into the other half of their cycle beyond man's range of sensing.

MAN'S INDIVIDUALITY

Man's greatest difficulty in comprehending "what happens after he disappears in death" is due to lack of comprehension of his immortality which never disappears. His visible body would be useless if it were not centered by his invisible, immortal Self, Soul, or Person.

Man is aware of himself as an individual, but his concept of what constitutes his individuality is vague. His individuality is what he unknowingly interprets his immortal Self to be. His Self, or Soul, never changes, never appears or disappears, but his individuality constantly changes to forever fit the changing concept of what he interprets his immortal Self to be. As every man gradually comes to know the Light of his Self in him, his individuality changes by the constant uplift toward that increasing awareness of his centering omniscience.

As greater awareness of the Light of the Universal Self comes to man, he gradually loses his individuality and becomes more that Universal Self. When mankind has become fully aware of God in him, the play of man on this planet is finished, his purpose fulfilled, and the individual man ceases to be.

Man loses his expression of life in matter—to find eternal life in the Light.

THERE IS NO DEATH.

"Know thou that divided lights which record My knowing are lights of suns, and darkness born of suns. All imaged forms of My all-knowing are born from dark to light, and mirrored back to dark for endless borning into light.

"Within still centers of My suns is My all-knowing. The still Light of My knowing lights of My thinking interchange to manifest My knowing in moving forms of My imagining.

"Wherefore I scatter seed of My all-knowing throughout My Kingdom as light of many suns, and children of those many suns, to father-mother My all-knowing in moving forms of My imagining.

"And behold! each sun of My divided thinking fathers a whole universe of My imagining, giving light to its unfolding dark, to forever quicken dark by light.

"In this wise all quickened Idea of Me within heavens of earths and suns unfolds from dark wombs of earths to light of suns, to refold within tombs and wombs of earths for reborning unto heavens of earths and suns.

"In this wise is My desire to give fulfilled by equal taking of My giving for multiplied regiving.

"See thou that man well knoweth that I, the Father-Mother of My universe, center all his givings and his regivings and measure them with watchful eyes to balance them in Me.

"Say thou to him that his moving is My moving, for without Me he can in no wise move, e'en to manifest Me in his moving."

—*From* THE DIVINE ILIAD

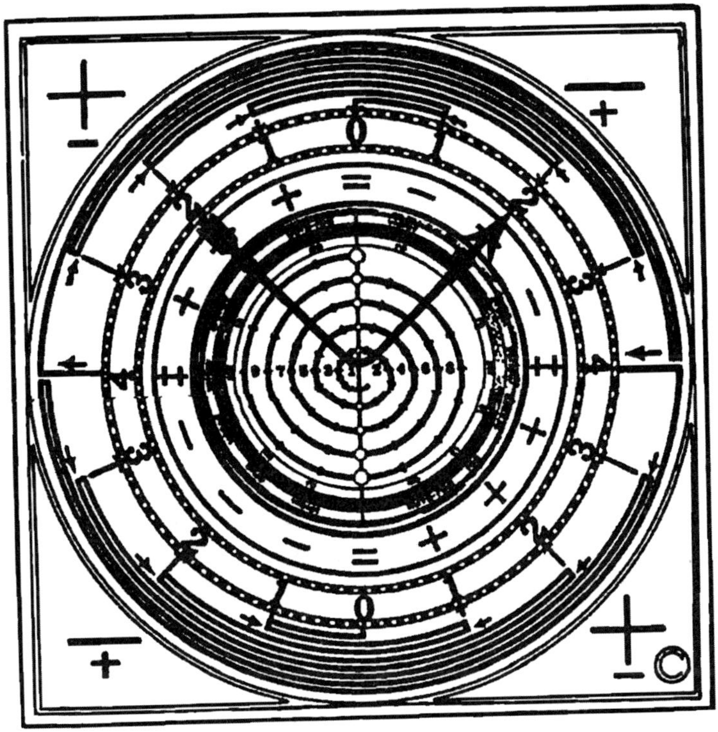

THE COSMIC CLOCK

THE SECRET OF LIGHT

Part III

The Mystery of

Gravitation and Radiation

OMNIPRESENCE

The Universe of Being

"In My universe there is but one form from which all forms appear. That one form is the pulsing cube-sphere, two halves of the heart-beat of My dual thinking.

"All forms pulse, therefore, all forms are two, one form for the inbreathing pulse, which generates, and one for the outbreathing, radiating one. The cube is the sphere expanded by the outward breath to black rest in cold space, and the sphere is the cube compressed to the incandescence of white-hot suns by the inward breath.

"All spheres emerge from the pulsing, breathing cubes of space and return to them to find fulcrums of rest for re-emergence.

"Behold, I center one form where it seeks rest in Me from the action of My thinking, and I envelop that form with its other half where it may again find rest in Me as another fulcrum for expression of My thinking.

"These two sexed halves extend from Me and return to Me, but they are not Me, nor are they two halves of one, for they never can be two halves of one. They are always two, and never one. Nor can they unite, nor meet, for their ways are opposed ways which never meet, for each one voideth each in their seeming meeting.

"Behold, I am within all things, centering them; and I am without all things, controlling them. But I am not those things which I center and control."

—*From* THE DIVINE ILIAD

"See thou that man knows that each divided light of his conditioning, which extends from Me to him, is balanced always, for I am Balance. And that is Truth and the Law, for I am Truth and the Law.

"Say thou to him: each thing is everything and each is everywhere.

"For I say that all things are the same thing, for all things are universal. Each thing reaches through every other thing to the farthermost star. For this purpose have I set My mirrors and My lenses of dual light to attain an infinity in My imaged universe in which no measure is.

"And I also say that man's infinity ends in eyes of man where it began. All things in My mirrored universe end where they began. Eternity thus ends in NOW, and Now in Eternity.

"See thou that man well knows the illusions which deceive his sense seeing. Point out to him My mirrors and my lenses which curve My universe of seeming into imaged spheres of My thinking as seed for multiplying One into many ones.

"Say thou to him: all things occupy the same space, and each thing occupies all space. All things extend from all things and are extensions of all things. Likewise I say: all things center all things and are involved in all things. *same space, and each thing occupies all space. All things extend from all things and are extensions of all things. Likewise I say: all things center all things and are involved in all things.*

"Say thou these things in words of man's knowing. And say thou that I, the Light, center him and all things else, for I am everywhere."

—*From* THE DIVINE ILIAD

"Again I say that all things extend to all things, from all things, and through all things. For, to thee I again say, all things are Light, and Light separates not; nor has it bounds; nor is it here and not there.

"Man may weave the pattern of his Self in Light of Me, and of his image in divided lights of Me, e'en as the sun sets up its bow of many hues from divided light of Me, but man cannot be apart from Me, as the spectrum cannot be apart from Light of Me.

hues from divided light of Me, but man cannot be apart from Me, as the spectrum cannot be apart from Light of Me.

"And as the rainbow is a light within the light, inseparable, so is Man's Self within Me, inseparable; and so is his image My image.

"Verily I say, every wave encompasseth every other wave unto the One; and the many are within the One, e'en down to the least of waves of Me.

"And I say further that every thing is repeated within every other thing, unto the One.

"And furthermore I say, that every element which man thinketh of as of itself alone is within every other element, e'en to the atom's veriest unit.

"When man queries thee in this wise: 'Sayest thou that in this iron there is gold and all things else?' thou may'st answer: 'Within the sphere, and encompassing it, is the cube, and every other form that is; and within the cube, and encompassing it, is the sphere, and every other form that is.' "

—*From* THE DIVINE ILIAD

THIS MAGNETIC-ELECTRIC UNIVERSE

IN POSTULATES AND DIAGRAMS

God is Light. God is Love.

God's creating universe is founded on Love. It is creating with Light.

The principle of love is desire to give. God gives love by extending His Light. God's love is a mirror of Light which reflects His giving of love by the regiving of love.

The law of love is rhythmic balanced interchange between all givings and regivings.

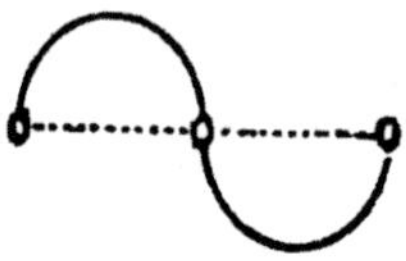

Fig. 1
Symbol of love extended from rest to motion

The symbol of love is the wave of dual light which gives and regives equally and rhythmically. This is a dual electric wave universe of interchanging light. (Fig. 1)

God's Love is everywhere; His Light is everywhere. There is naught but good in God's omniscient universe. Evil is a product of man's thinking.

God extends His love, His power and His knowing, radially, from zero points of omnipresent stillness to other zero points in the measure of His desire to give form to His imaginings. The intensity of desire extended from centering points of rest to extended points of rest determines the dimension of desire. (Fig. 2)

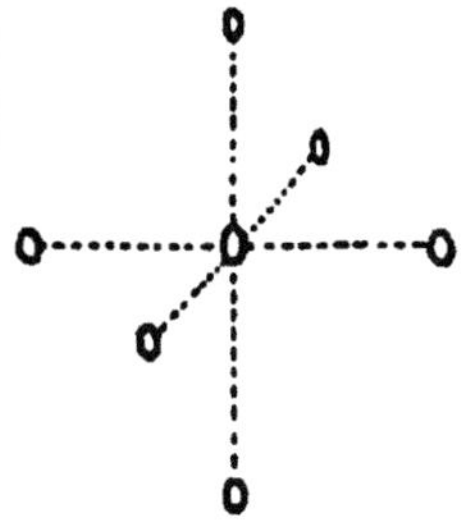

Fig. 2
Symbol of power extended from rest to rest

THIS RADIAL UNIVERSE

The entire mechanical principal of Nature, by means of which its light illusions of motion are produced, is the consequent effect of such radial extensions. Because of it, the seeming multiplication and division of the universal equilibrium into the opposed electrical pressures of gravitation and radiation, which form the foundation of this universe of change, are made possible. (Fig. 3)

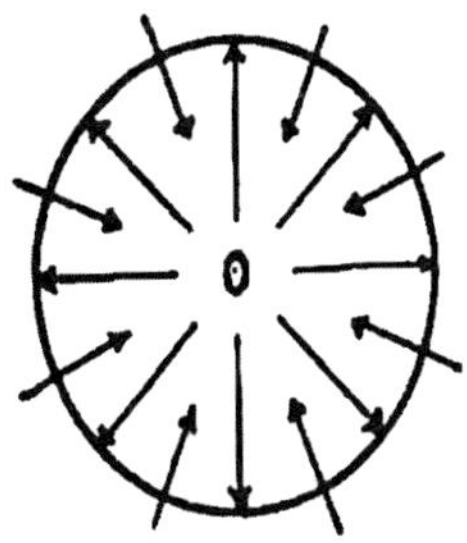

Fig. 3
The radial universe

God's imaginings extend from rest to rest in His three-dimensional radial universe of length, breadth and thickness—to become the stage of space for His imagined radial universe of matter, time, change and motion. (Fig. 4)

Points of rest, further extended to other points of rest, form three reflecting planes of still magnetic Light which are at right angles to each other. (Fig. 4) From the center of these three mirror planes of zero curvature, God's givings are radially projected to six opposed mirror planes for reprojection as regivings, to unfold

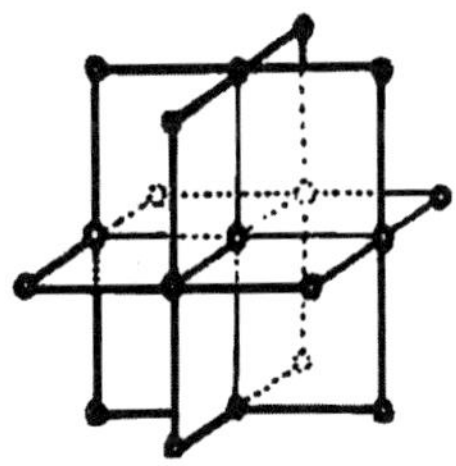

Fig. 4
God's projection mirrors of action

and refold the forms of God's imaginings in the curved electric universe of His desiring. (Fig. 5)

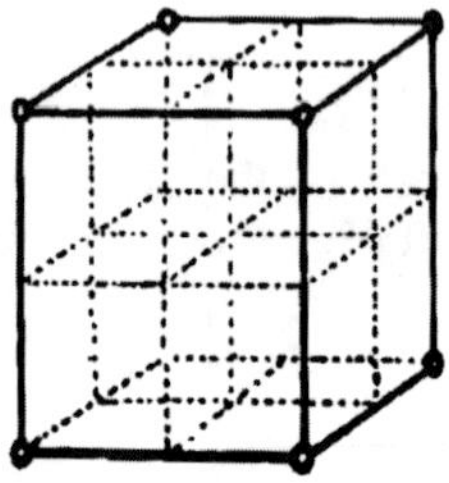

Fig. 5
Mirror planes of reaction

BIRTH OF WAVE FIELDS

The desire of God to give of His love is manifested in projected action as an outward explosion from a centering point of rest acting as a fulcrum. The desire to regive is simultaneously "radarred" back from every point of its progress to refold the unfolding action. All action in Nature is forever disappearing into a mirror of its own image of equal potential. (Figs. 5 and 6)

Fig. 6
The explosive action

Every projected action in Nature which is *simultaneously* "radarred" back as a reprojected reaction is *sequentially* repeated as a similar echo from its wave field boundary planes of zero curvature. (Fig. 7)

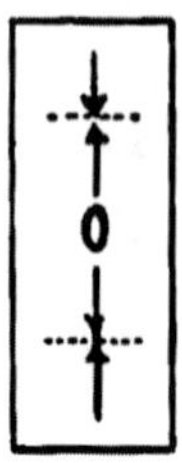

Fig. 7
Simultaneous reactions

All actions in Nature are outward explosions—slow actions of growing things, or fast actions of released dynamite or atom bomb. Conversely, all reactions are inward explosions. Actions unfold formlessness into form. Reactions refold form into formlessness. Actions are the basis of radiation. Reactions are the basis of gravitation. (Fig. 8)

Every action anywhere is repeated every where throughout the universe. As a consequence, harmonic centers of the same measure of desire extend their actions outward from their centers toward other harmonic centers. Harmonic explosions of equal measure thus fill all space in God's omnipresent universe. (Fig. 9)

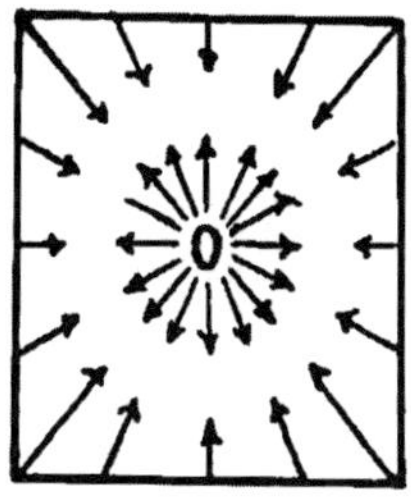

Fig. 8
Sequential reaction

Outward explosions which meet each other cannot be spheres, for all space must be filled. Tennis balls crushed together become cubes by gradually flattening where they meet at six points on curved surfaces. Likewise, outer explosions flatten into the six planes of cubes. (Fig. 10)

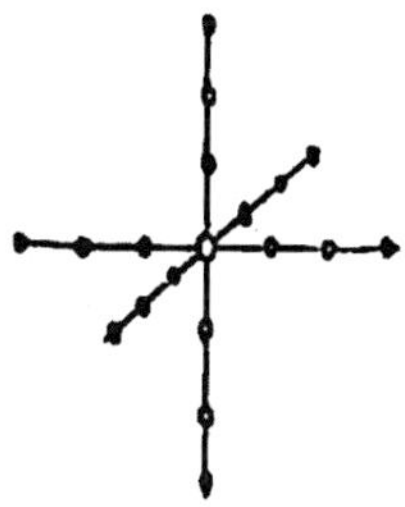

Fig. 9
All action is omnipresent

Outward-inward explosions are resisted at their maximum in the direction of the six points where spheres meet. They are consequently deflected to the eight points of least resistance which become diagonals of cubes instead of radii of spheres. (Fig. 11)

Eight directions of two-way expressed force are thus generated which become the basis of the octave wave. (Fig. 12)

Fig. 10
Repeated explosions meet

Outward-inward explosions projected through each other develop two opposed pressures. The outward direction divides its potential by expanding it radially. The inward direction mul-

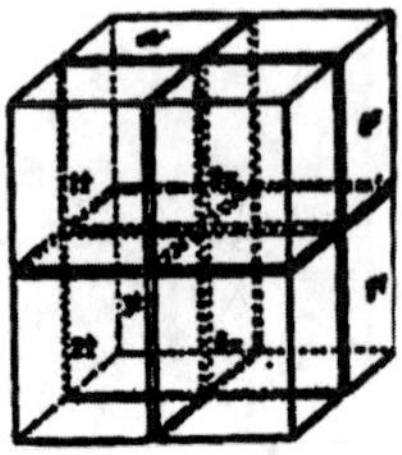

Fig. 11
Repeated explosions compress

tiplies it by compressing it radially. Thus, the two opposite plus and minus equilibrium conditions are produced which motivate this electric universe of two-way motion, give to it its heartbeat and produce all effects of illusion caused by the interchange of the two conditions of matter.

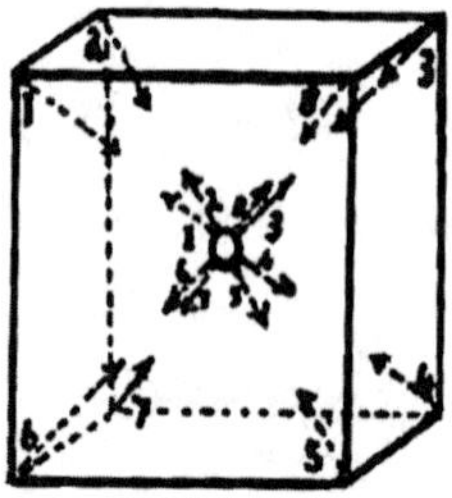

Fig. 12
The eight two-way directions of force

THE CUBE-SPHERE

Pairs of interchanging opposed conditions are born from each other and become each other as a consequence of that interchange, as all opposites in Nature are likewise born. The cube and the sphere are the two opposites of form from which all forms of all things are born. They are the only forms ever created, being father-mother of all forms. (Figs. 13,14)

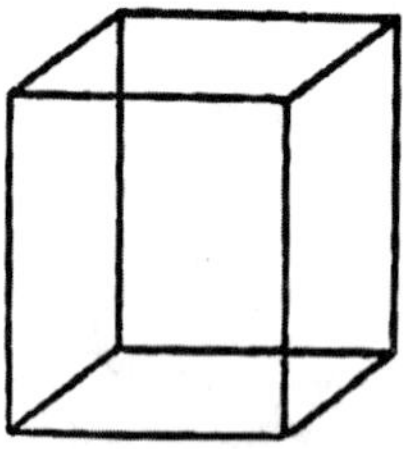

Fig. 13
The cube

The sphere and the cube both manifest the cosmic principle of balance. Their position in light waves is in the one balanced position in the wave where compression and expansion have ceased to oppose each other, which is at wave amplitude (known as trough or crest). Carbon and sodium chloride are good examples of true cube crystallization. Likewise their atomic units are true spheres. Sodium-iodide or sodium-bromide do not crystallize in true cube because of their unbalanced positions near, but not upon, the plane of wave amplitude.

Fig. 14
The Sphere

The cube and sphere are one, being two opposite phases of the same thing. The cube is the sphere extended to black coldness while the sphere is the cube contracted to white incandescence. Every true sphere in every light wave is an incandescent sun, regardless of its dimension. Prolating spheres, such as our sun, are becoming incandescent inward toward their centers, while oblating spheres, such as our planets, are becoming cold inward toward their centers.

The cube is born from the sphere to fulfill the desire of the Creator to produce form by projecting light from incandescence toward the cold dark of the heavens. Conversely, the sphere is born from the cube to fulfill the other desire for oneness by reprojecting cold dark from the heavens to light in the seed.

The creation of all forms of matter is an eternal interchange between the father-light of incandescent spheres and the mother-light of cold cubes. All forms are born in the direction of the coldness of space and are voided in the direction of incandescence.

Every creating body is set out into space from its crucible in the sun to cool into the form appropriate to its extension from the sun. That is one half of the cyclic

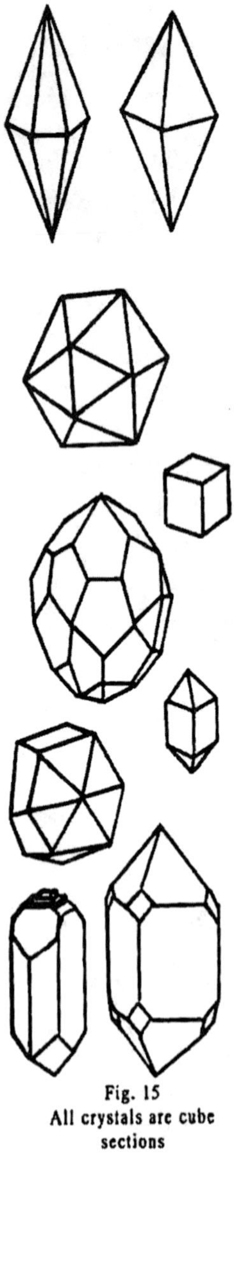

Fig. 15
All crystals are cube sections

journey of every body from the sun and back to it. The other half of the cycle is the return to the sun to void the body of its form for the purpose of acquiring a new body. Every cycle of motion is a journey from heat to cold and back again.

All bodies are *formed* by *freezing* and *voided* by melting. The freezing and melting points of all bodies are dependent upon their respective densities and electric conditioning.

The sphere is the clay of earths, the light of suns and the formlessness of seed. It is the womb from which the clay of earth extends into the cube-bound heavens to expand into form, and it is the tomb within which all form is voided for regiving to the heavens as a new form.

Every form in Nature is either becoming a cube or a sphere, or is a section of either one. Complex bodies are multiples of spheres of matter surrounded by multiples of cubes of space in multiples of wave fields. All crystal shapes are sections of cubes. Their shapes are determined by their positions in their wave field. (Fig. 15)

The cubes of space are wave fields which bound all interchanging motion between the two conditions within it. Motion cannot pass through these planes but can be reflected symmetrically back or extended symmetrically toward the center of the adjoining wave field.

Within each cube field is the curved universe of two-way light illusion; and beyond, to the farthest reaches of space, is a repetition of illusion from wave field to wave field at the rate of 186,400 miles per second. That is the speed in which every action-reaction anywhere repeats itself everywhere. This illusion of motion gives rise to the belief that light "travels."

Wave field boundary planes of zero curvature insulate all effects of motion, which take place within it, from every other wave field. Centering the wave field is the incandescent sphere which mates it. The potential of the entire field is divided equally between its centering sphere of *multiplied* matter and the surrounding space of *divided* matter.

Each mate of each wave field in the universe is balanced with its opposite mate, even to the weight of one electron. The reason why the centering sphere is of high potential and its surrounding space is of low potential is due to a difference of volume. The centering sphere may be a few thousand miles in diameter and its surrounding space many millions of miles in diameter; yet they are equal, potential for potential, but unequal volume for volume.

Neither of these mates could sustain its separateness of condition unless it constantly interchanged to give all of itself to the other alternately in repetitive cycles. Spheres must give to cubes of space by breathing out to discharge themselves and charge space. Space must then regive to spheres by breathing out from itself to discharge itself and recharge spheres.

Each short cycle of interchange is accumulated into a longer life-death cycle in which solids entirely disappear into space and space interchanges its potential to become solids. This principle constitutes the forever inside-out outside-in turnings of Nature by means of which all forms sequentially appear, disappear and reappear.

The inbreathing of spheres generates low potential into high. The generative process of Nature is gravitation. The outbreathing of spheres radiates high potential into low. The degenerative process of Nature is radiation.

Multiplication and division of expressed energy into the high and low potential of gravitation and radiation is made possible by the plan of Nature which causes all actions of Nature to extend radially from omnipresent points of magnetic Light.

Gravitation pulls spirally inward from within to wind light waves into solids to center space.[2] Radiation thrusts spirally outward to unwind dense solids into space to surround solids. Each is an equal reaction of the other. Each becomes the other sequentially.

Gravitation is the positive electric principle which exerts its pressures centripetally toward the maximum incandescent points of compression in every wave field. It is the father principle of Nature, the integrating principle of "uphill flow of energy" which forever balances its "downhill flow."

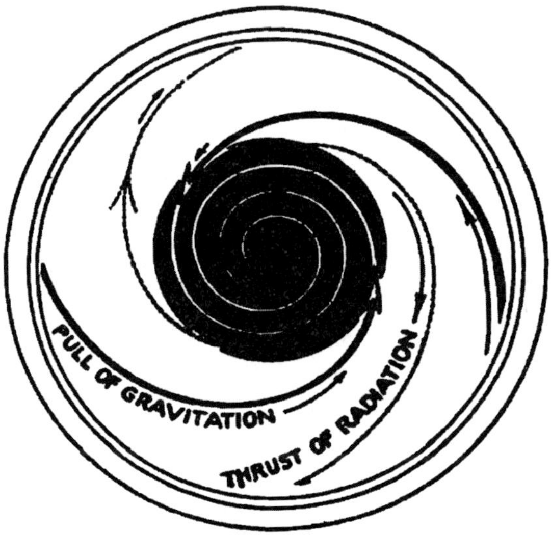

Fig. 16

The Mystery of Gravitation and Radiation[2]

Radiation is the negative electric principle which exerts its pressures centrifugally toward its wave field boundary planes of magnetic Light. It is the mother principle of Nature, the disintegrating principle of "downhill flow of energy" which forever balances its "uphill flow."

The Creator extends power of motion to but one half of a cycle for each of the two opposite manifestations of His desire. Gravity gives a material form to bodies to manifest the idea of bodies. Radioactivity gives spiritual formlessness to the heavens for regiving to earths as formed bodies.

Gravity begins its half cycle as the inward explosive reaction of an outward explosive action, thus fulfilling the law that all opposite expressions are born from each other and interchange to become the other. It ends its half cycle at a point of rest at the still point of magnetic light which centers every material body whether of microcosmic or macrocosmic dimension. Gravity then ceases when its motion ceases.

There is no "center of gravity" in Nature. The centering Light of every mass is still magnetic Light. Likewise the still axis of every vortex is still magnetic Light.

Radiativity then begins its half cycle from that point of rest and ends it on wave field boundary planes of magnetic Light where gravity began. Radiativity then ceases when its motion ceases.

Both gravity and radiativity borrow their power to find balance in rest at their journey's end from the points of rest of their beginnings. They each repay their separate borrowings to the other at every point of their respective journeys. Each thus perpetually voids itself by giving to the other. At each journey's end, each opposite cancels itself out by giving its all to the other. *It is then reborn as the other.* Everywhere in Nature each action is its own reaction.

"Death gives to life that life may live; and life gives to death that death may die."

—*From* THE DIVINE ILIAD

Every action in Nature demonstrates this principle. A ball thrown in the air must start from a point of rest, motivated by energy borrowed from the "center of gravity" of this earth which is its fulcrum. The point of rest in the thrower's hand is an extension of the earth's still center.

As the ball ascends, it decelerates as it pays its borrowed energy to space, thus charging space with the borrowings of earth and equally discharging earth. When the borrowing is fully paid the ball comes to rest. From that point it must again borrow the energy from space which it borrowed from earth to pay for its return to earth. Upon its accelerative journey to earth it passes each point at the same speed it registered on the upward half cycle, thus discharging space and equally charging earth to balance all borrowings and payings.

All actions in Nature are extension-retractions from zero to zero, and back again to zero. All are balanced simultaneously and sequentially. This is a zero universe of plus and minus zero which never exceeds the zero of the One Light from which it seemingly sprang as multiplicity.

THE TWO OPPOSITE ELECTRIC CONDITIONS

This zero universe of equilibrium demands two opposed conditions in order to simulate that which our senses interpret for motion and change. These two needed conditions are plus and minus equilibrium; positive and negative electricity. (Fig. 17)

Plus zero means a credit of pressure borrowed from the universal equilibrium to compress a large volume into a small volume. Minus zero means an equal expansion to balance the borrowed compression.

Fig. 17
X plus zero equals zero minus X

A thousand dollars borrowed from a bank is a plus condition of credit which is balanced by an equal debit of one thousand dollars. The central zero represents the bank. The extended zeros represent credit and debit. Both are equal but opposite. A credit of one thousand dollars equals zero. When the credit is paid in part or in full the debit is proportionately voided simultaneously with the credit.

These two opposite conditions of credit and debit correspond with the two opposite conditions of compression and expansion in Nature upon which motion is dependent. When an equilibrium pressure is divided into opposite conditions from the zero from which both are extended, motion between the two becomes imperative. They must interchange with each other to void their unbalanced conditions. *This is the principle of the electric current.*

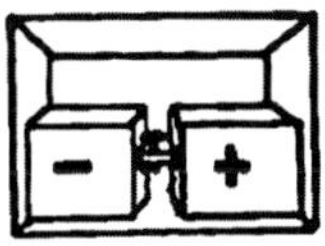

Fig. 18
Basis of Motion

Fig. 18 represents a room of equal pressure. Two tanks in it are connected with a tube and petcock. By pumping all the air out of one tank into the other, the two plus-minus conditions have been established which make motion imperative. Nature always borns each opposite from the other in this manner.

Fig. 18
Basis of Motion

By opening the petcock an outward explosion will take place in the plus tank. An inward explosion of equal potential will take place in the evacuated tank. The plus tank will *discharge* part of its compressed condition to *charge* the minus one. The electric battery is the same in principle. (Fig. 19)

Fig. 19
Equal opposite potentials

In Nature the discharged radiation which explodes outward from the sun simultaneously explodes inward as gravitation.

CAUSE OF THE UNIVERSAL PULSE BEAT

Matter and space constitute the two conditions necessary for interchange of motion diagrammed in Figs. 18 and 19 with one distinguishing difference. That difference is that the two conditions represented by the tanks of the compressed and expanded air and the two cells of the electric battery are *equal in volume,* while bodies of matter and their surrounding space are *unequal in volume.*

The expanded condition of space is millions of times greater in volume than the compressed condition of its centering body.

This explains the seeming mystery of gravitation and radiation which causes solid objects to fall toward the earth and gases to rise toward space.

In the electric battery the interchange between the two pressure conditions can void both in an explosive flash by a short circuit if the wire connecting both cells is heavy enough. If a small wire connects both cells the interchange takes time to complete the voidance. Each condition gives to the other in installments, for the wire is not big enough to void both conditions instantly. The consequent giving and regiving by the two opposite pressures constitute the oscillations of the electric current. Electric interchange by installments is measured and recorded by waves, and the time element of those recordings of interchange are wave frequencies. They constitute the pulse beat of the electric current. When an electric wire pulses with wave frequencies of an electric current we say that it is a live wire. When it stops pulsing because the current is disconnected we say that the wire is dead, for it no longer pulses.

All Nature pulses in measured frequencies with the heartbeat of the universal electric current, as evidenced by universal breathing inward toward bodies and outward toward space. When breathing is switched off in man's body by the cessation of interchange between the two opposite pressure conditions of matter, we say that the man is dead. By solving the mystery of "installment interchange" between bodies and space one can more fully comprehend the fact that neither pulse beat, breathings nor wave frequencies of interchange have any relation whatsoever to life, for they relate only to the principle by means of which life or energy is manifested by motion.

The first step in solving this mystery lies in the principle by means of which matter and space become unequal in volume.

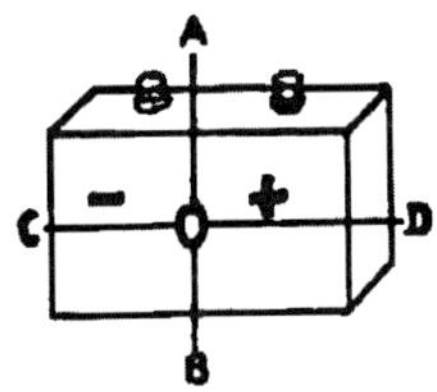

Fig. 20
Balanced interchange between equal conditions

Fig. 20 represents the electric battery with the line AB dividing the two pressure conditions as the equilibrium of both. This line represents *a static equator*—a plane of rest from which both

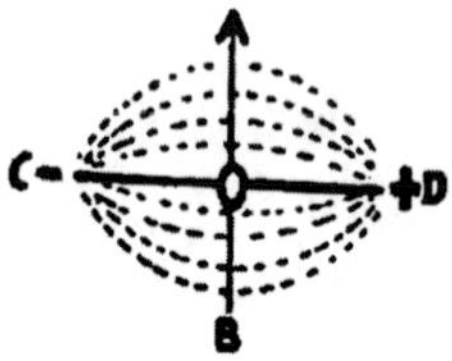

Fig. 21
Symmetry of the cube
AB Static equator CD
Dynamic equator

opposite conditions are extended at right angles as *a dynamic equator*—line CD.

Fig. 21 represents static and dynamic equators (or magnetic and electric) at ninety degrees from each other. As the two opposed conditions which extend from these planes of rest are equal, the lines of force which connect both are as symmetrical to both diameters as though reflected by mirrors placed at right angles to each other. Such symmetry belongs to the cube and sphere alone.

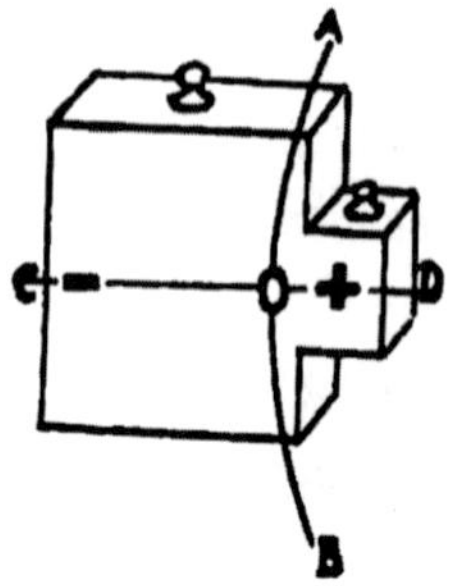

Fig. 22
Interchange between unequal opposites

Fig. 22 represents the electric battery with the negative cell much larger than the positive cell. The static and dynamic equators will still be at right angles to each other but the static equator *will not be in the middle.* It will be much nearer the positive pole and *will be curved* because lines of force which record the measure of interchange between the two opposite pressures can be symmetrical to the dynamic equator only, and not to the static equator.

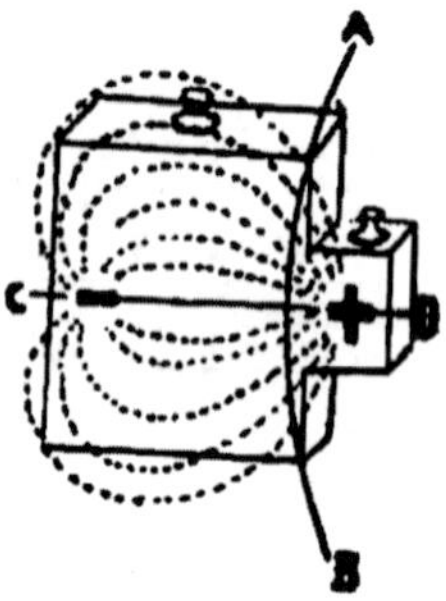

Fig. 23
Curvature increases

Such symmetry belongs to the radial universe of cone sections. All dynamic equators are radial, and all lines of force of conic symmetry are forever changing to record the forever changing potential of dynamic equators.

Fig. 23 illustrates this principle which forms spheres and creates the illusion which makes heavy objects seem to be attracted radially toward the earth and tenuous matter thrust radially away from it. Line AB shows the curvature of the static equator which causes the dynamic equator to expand at its negative end and contract at its positive end into the radii of a cone. The outward thrust of radiative pressures would curve the base of the cone thus produced to correspond with the curvature of its static equator, AB.

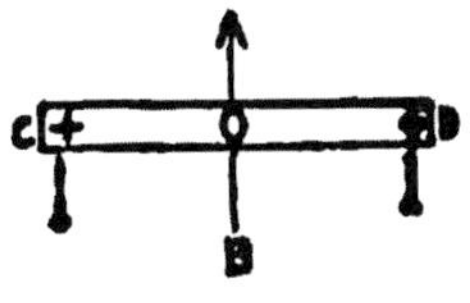

Fig. 24
Equal interchange

Fig. 24 represents a bar magnet which has been divided into the two opposite pressure conditions of this electric universe by coiling a charged wire around the bar of steel, thus forming two opposed plus and minus electrical vortices with intensities measured at poles.

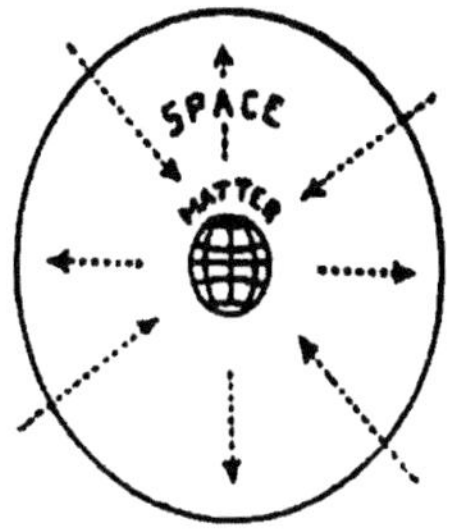

Two nails of equal weight are suspended to these poles. It is not magnetism, however, which picks up these nails. It is the electric vortices which pick them up, for the vortices are still effective upon that steel bar even though the electrically charged wire has been removed.

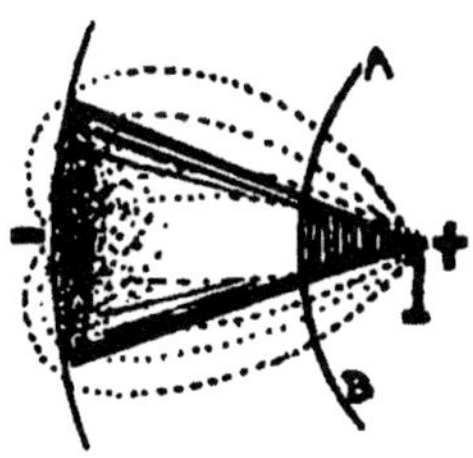

Fig. 25 A & B
Interchange between unequal volumes

It is the whirlpool motion of the electric vortex which performs the work of lifting those nails and not the stillness of the poles of magnetic Light.

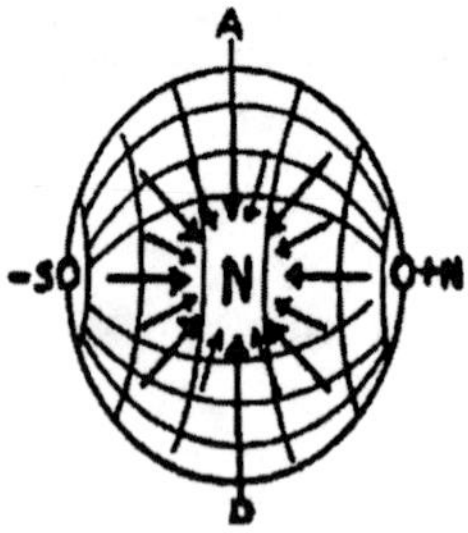

Fig. 26

If the bar magnet is enlarged at one end it becomes a cone. The division into the two opposed conditions will still be equal, as in Fig. 25, but the volume will bė so large in one as compared with the other that the nail which the positive end will still pick up cannot be lifted by the negative end unless the nail is ground to a fine powder. The negative end will then lift the same weight in total but only by dividing the nail over the whole volume.

Before this principle is applied to matter and space, it is necessary to correct the general impression that the earth is a magnet. By referring to the bar magnet pictured in Fig. 24 it can be seen that its poles alone express gravity. The earth, on the contrary, expresses gravity at its center. (Fig. 26)

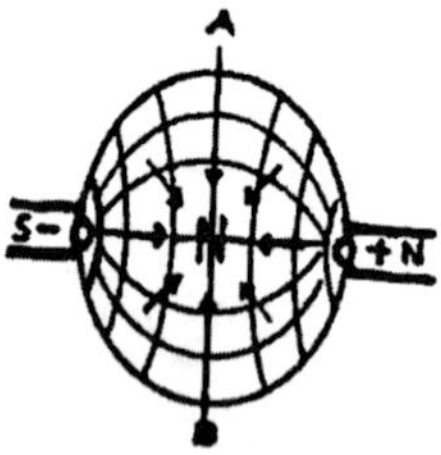

Fig. 27
Matter is formed between opposite poles in waves

The earth is formed between magnetic gaps of its wave as all bodies are formed (Fig. 27). If two bar magnets are placed so that negative and positive ends are near each other, that still point which we call the center of gravity will evidence itself between the two ends. If iron filings are placed in this gap, conditions of gravity similar to those of the earth will be found there.

Gravity will end and radiation will begin at that center. Nails will fall toward it from any direction, as heavy objects do on earth, and compass needles will follow the vortical directions of lines of force which extend toward its poles.

The analogy between the unequal battery cells and bar magnets is now sufficiently complete to compare them with matter and space. In Fig. 28 two bar magnets have been fanned out into cones. The weight which the positive end will pick up as a solid has to be finely divided in order for the expanded volume of the negative end to pick it up.

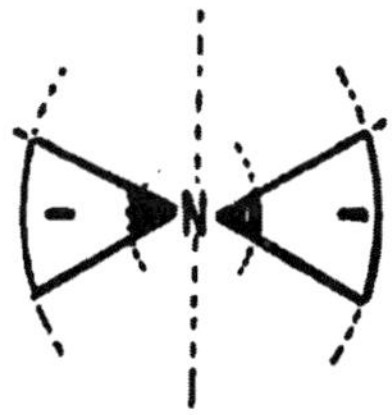

Fig. 28
Curvature increases as potentials divide and multiply

The essential difference between the two opposed pressure conditions of the electric battery and the two of matter and space is that in the battery the opposed potentials are equal because the volumes are equal.

In the universal battery of matter and space the two opposed conditions are conspicuously *unequal*. The resultant high and low potential contrast each other so violently that solid matter "falling" toward the high potential of the compressed condition must be divided into vapors and gases before the same substance will "fall" toward the low potential of the expanded condition. A solid bar of iron will *fall* radially toward the earth because both are high potential compressed solids. If divided sufficiently by vaporizing it, that same bar of iron will *fall* radially toward the heavens.

Gravity and radiativity are opposite pressure *conditions* of the same thing. Both of those pressure conditions are in every creating thing. Every creating thing can expand to lower its potential, or can contract to raise it. Like conditions seek like conditions to find balance. Creating things changing their compressed conditions to expanded conditions must move to find balance in like conditions. That is the sole cause of two-way motion.

Every potential has a balancing potential position somewhere in the universe. Desire to find that position is in every creating thing and any restraint exerted to prevent it from moving to find its balancing potential can be measured as weight.

The cause of the radial universe which constitutes matter and space lies in the inequality of its two opposite pressure conditions both as to volume and potential.

The cause of the universal pulse beat and the breathing which motivates the manifestation of life in every creating thing lies also in this inequality. All creating things pulse and breathe just as organic "life" pulses and breathes, but that is not *life;* it is but *motion.*

THE TWO OPPOSITE ELECTRIC DIRECTIONS

The universe is dual—the still magnetic universe of reality and the *dynamic* electric, radial two-way universe of illusion which extends from the static universe at an angle of ninety degrees.

In the dynamic electric universe there are two directions—inward and outward radially from a still *point* of magnetic Light to still *planes* of magnetic Light. All motion within magnetic wave fields is controlled by the Creator. (Figs. 29, 30)

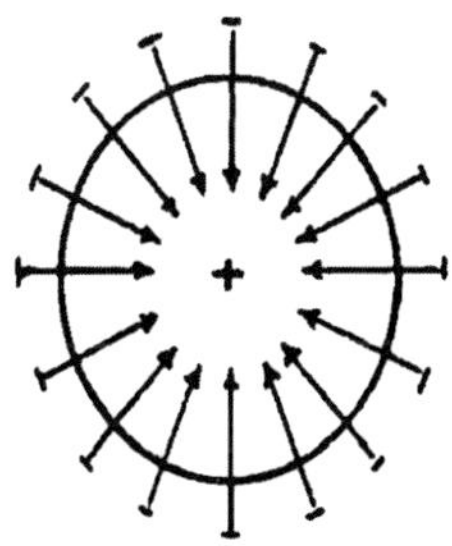

Fig. 29
North

"For behold, I am within all things, centering them, and I am without all things, controlling them."—From THE DIVINE ILIAD

The inward radial direction is North—the compressive direction of gravity which multiplies potential by compressing light waves radially into smaller volumes of greater frequencies. The outward radial direction is South—the expansive direction of radiation which divides potential by expanding light waves into larger volumes of lesser frequencies. (Fig. 31)

Fig. 30
South

The two directions of the static universe are

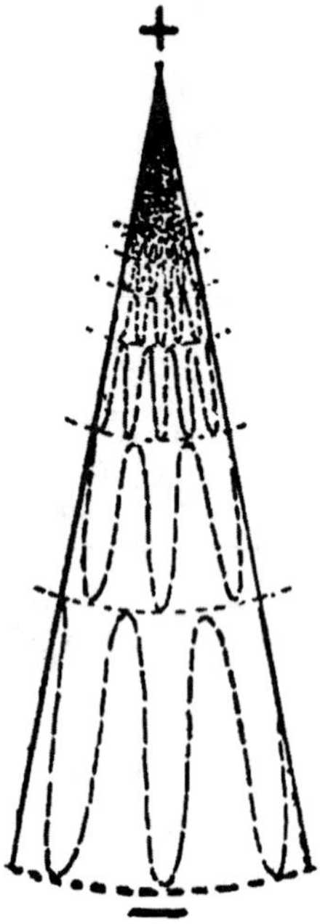

Fig. 31
The division and multiplication principle

East and West. They are static because they are spherical. They follow curved planes of unchanging equipotential pressures, such as the contour of the earth or sun or of the orbits of planets or floating clouds. East and West do not oppose each other. Each arrives at its own starting point without change of potential. (Fig. 32)

North and South, on the contrary, diametrically oppose each other. They are constantly changing. They seek opposite directions, each passing *through* the other in opposite spiral lanes; each interchanging with the other as it passes; each voiding the other through that interchange, and each becoming the other because of it. (Fig. 33)

East-West spherical planes form the axes of light waves from which the dynamic universe extends its gyroscopic wave, radially, at amplitudes of ninety degrees and also its other gyroscopic octave tones at the varying degrees of pressures where the elements of matter are formed.

East-West spherical planes are also the fulcrums of wave levers which curve gravity as they pump high potential into low to expand solids into the gases of space, and low potential into high to compress light waves into the solids of earths. (Fig. 34)

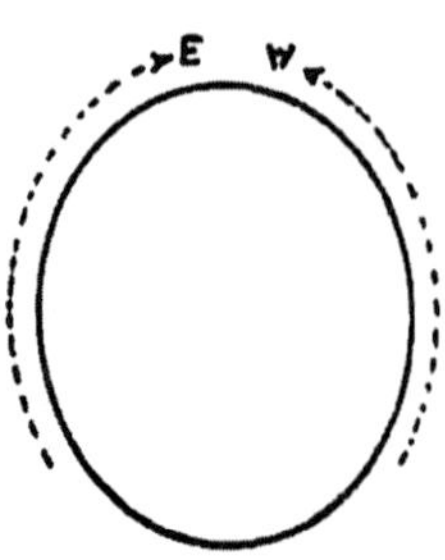

Fig. 32

Incandescent suns of white hot light are born from cold black darkness and cold dark space is born from white hot suns.

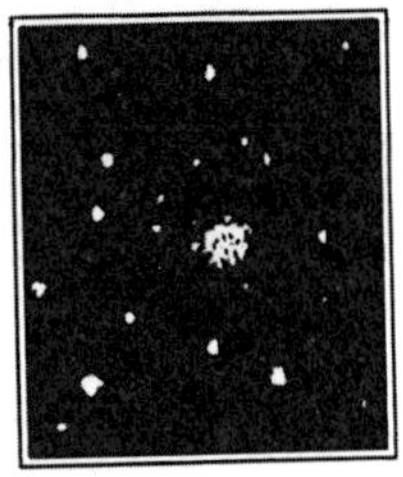

Fig. 33

THIS CURVED ELECTRIC UNIVERSE

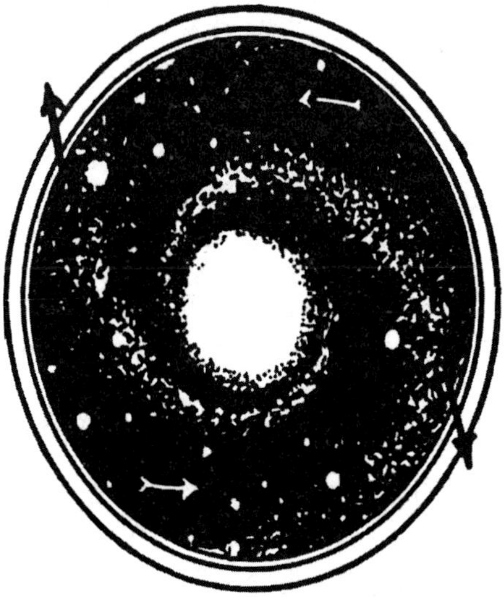

Fig. 35
Light comes from darkness and darkness from light

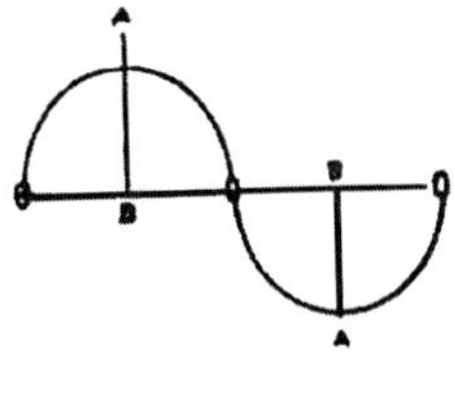

Fig 34

All suns are *generated* into incandescence by two black rivers of evacuated light which flow centripetally inward toward their still centers by the way of their poles. Conversely, darkness of space is *radiated* from two incandescent rivers of white light which flow centrifugally from suns' equators. (Fig. 35)

Fig. 36 and 37

Thus are the four arms of all spiral nebulae formed as two pairs of opposites interchanging with each other to become the other two; the two black arms belong to gravity and the two white ones to vacuity. (Figs. 36, 37, 38)

Fig. 38
The four rivers of light

This electric universe is curved—motion is spiral. Where motion ceases, curvature ceases. Cleavages between wave field boundary planes of crystals separate them into their individual crystal forms. Motion cannot pass through those planes, for there is naught but stillness there. Motion is repeated in all wave fields by reflected extension from wave field boundary planes.

Curvature is imperative under such conditions for opposed pressures resist each other and each must bend to the other to find passage for its own expression of force. *Motion and curvature simultaneously begin and end when opposition begins and ends.* (Zero in Fig. 39)

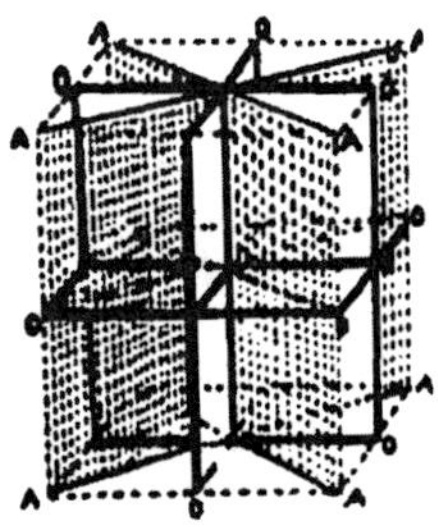

Fig. 39
O-Mirror planes of still light
A-Screen of space for projected lights of motion

Each wave field is like a separate projection machine in which its own curved motion picture universe is dually projected upon its self-measured zero screen of space. (A in Fig. 39). The incandescent sphere of light which centers it pictures the forms of desire in the measure of desire for manifestation. (See also Fig. 38)

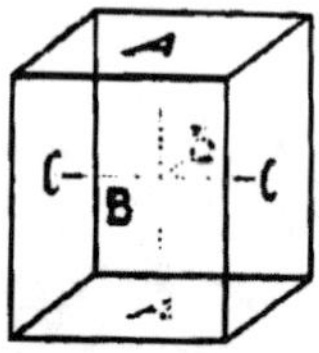

Fig. 40
The six wave field boundary planes

This curved universe consists of lenses and mirrors of light which reflect, bend, curve, concentrate and decentrate light into its countless forms. Any action anywhere is repeated everywhere by and through countless mirror planes of wave fields and the lenses of space. (Figs. 40, 41)

Fig. 41
The universe of projected motion

Concentrated spheres, such as the earth and sun, are surrounded by layers of light of equal pressures. Clouds float around the earth in them. The reason they float in curves parallel to the earth is because of these spherical equipotential planes of pressures which curve as the earth curves.

Curved pressures of light act as lenses to multiply and divide light radially. Light rays which pass through curved planes concentrate toward a point when projected through light lenses of space in the convex direction and decentrate when they pass through in the concave direction. (Figs. 42, 43)

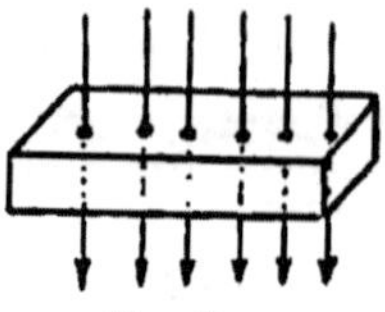
Fig. 42
Light rays are parallel when passing through planes of zero curvature

Gravity and radiativity are accounted for by this fact. Every object which falls toward the earth falls radially toward its center because of this fact. No two men who stand upright in balance with gravity stand parallel to each other. Lines drawn through the feet and head of any two men standing in either hemisphere would form a cone with its base in the heavens and its apex at earth's center. Rain falling vertically from a cloud falls conically. The area of the base of the cone in the cloud is greater than its conical measurement on the earth (Figs. 44, 45). The electric potential of rain increases as it falls because of the multiplication of pressures by the lenses of light which surround the earth. For the same reason a man weighs less as he ascends a mountain and regains it when descending. Light lenses subtract from his potential by multiplying its volume while he ascends and multiplies it while he descends by subtracting from its volume.

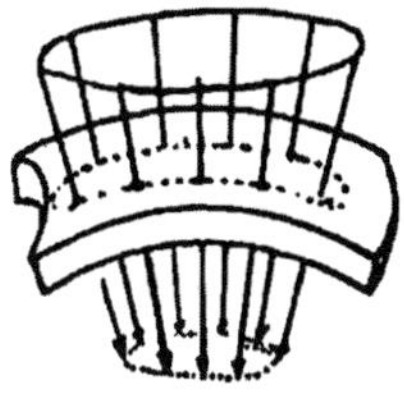

Fig. 43
Light rays are radial when projected through spherical planes

Curvature of light wave axes, by contraction or expansion between planes of zero curvature is the cause of all pressures; all pattern; all of the attributes of matter, such as density, tenuity, melting point, brittleness, conductivity and countless other effects which are voided when curvature ceases in planes of rest in wave field boundaries, or in points of rest around which motion rotates spirally.

Fig. 44
No two vertical lines are parallel in this radial universe
AA static equator

Fig. 45
Rain falling vertically forms cones

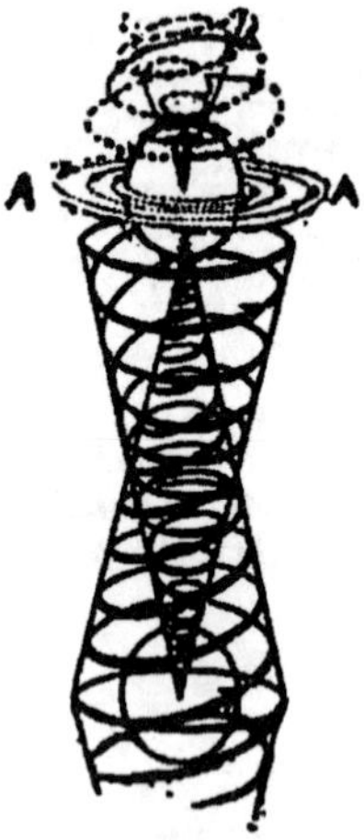

Fig. 50
AA Birth of electronic systems

Fig. 51
Spiral Mates. Units of electric current

are born where centripetal and centrifugal spirals meet. Matter registers the potential of the position of its birth. For that reason it floats in equipotential orbits appropriate to its position in its wave field, together with all units of its system. In the electric current, electronic systems are born where the familiar loops of force occur around a charged wire (Fig. 50). Figs. 51, 52, and 53 diagram electric systems forming at AA.

The spiral is an incompleted sphere just as crystal forms are incompleted cubes. Spirals and crystals have individuality which they lose by voidance in the oneness of spheres and cubes.

Individuality is given bodies for the purpose of manifesting separateness and multiplicity. Individuality, separateness and multiplicity are then voided in oneness.

Individuality in every creating thing is a moment to moment record of its unfoldment and refoldment. It is the fruit of cosmic desire for creative expression. It begins when the cycle begins, ends with its ending, and repeats itself in each cycle until the entire cycle of any expressed idea is voided in its completion.

Two-way sex-conditioned spirals are the consummate individuals of all Creation. They condition all bodies with the condition of their bodies. They unfold all idea from stillness of Mind-knowing into moving form of Mind-imagining and refold it into the stillness of Mind-knowing. They are the electric workers which fulfill desire of Mind by interweaving threads of light into patterned forms and recording those patterned forms in the still Light which centers every spiral pair, as the axis of a cone centers the cone.

Fig. 52
Atomic systems forming

The one centering axis of both spirals is the shaft upon which the dynamic universe rotates.

All motion rotates and revolves upon still centering shafts, and all shafts are two-way extensions of points which lead to and through centers of spheres.

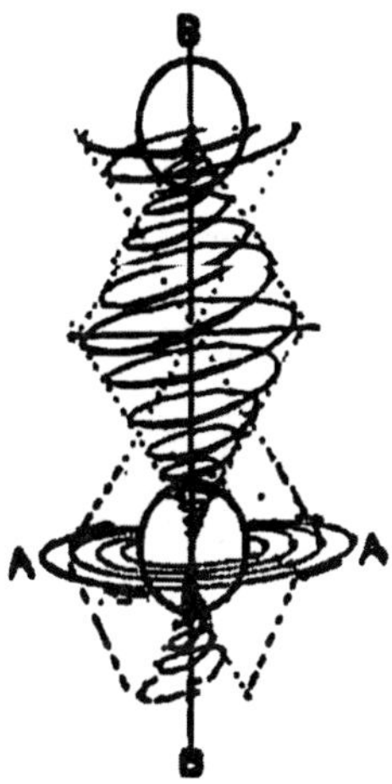

Fig. 53
AA Atomic systems forming
BB Wave shaft

The familiar wave line which records all effects of motion controls those effects. One can record that wave line but is not aware of the fact that it is the power extended by the Creator in the measure of desire for power.

The wave line is a record of the amount of energy borrowed from its static equator to express any mechanical process, such as the vibration of a harp string, the pulsations of an

Fig. 54

engine, the cardiogram of one's heartbeat, or the pattern of an earthquake, as recorded by a seismograph. (Figs. 54, 55, 56, 57, 58)

The shaft of a wave is a line drawn through every point upon the surface of a wave-disturbed ocean in a vertical section, where water and sky meet. Around the still shaft of the wave all motion of the wave spirals to interweave the patterns and forms of desire.

All spiral forms must have intense individuality in order to express such amazing varieties of form and pattern. (Fig. 59)

Fig. 55
AB—The shaft of earth and moon

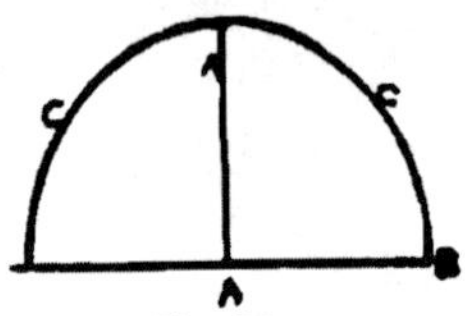

Fig. 56

Fig. 57
A—The measure of energy borrowed. B—Its repetition

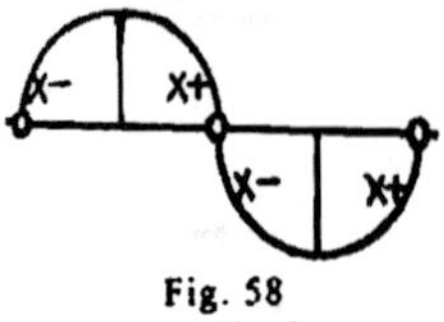

Fig. 58
A—is a credit. B—is an equal debit

The inside-out outside-in turnings of all creating forms is due to the gradual unfolding-refolding principle of Nature. This process is controlled by spiral pairs which are motivated by still centering shafts of magnetic Light. Opposed pairs of spirals gradually expand centrifugally to planes meeting at static equators to complete the unfolding half of a cycle. They then contract as the opposite of what they were to complete the other half. During the entire journey they continue without reversal of direction.

A clockwise spiral is always a clockwise spiral during its entire centripetal journey to its apex and its centrifugal journey to its base.

The opposed pair which rotate upon the same shaft are anticlockwise, *for both are projected through each other.* (Fig. 60)

The characteristic unfolding-refolding, inside-out outside-in principle of Nature causes the integration of matter at poles and disintegration at equators. Matter integrates by the contraction of one pair of spirals around the shafts which wind it into spheres by the way of their poles, and disintegrates it by the expansion of the other pair which unwind it by way of equators.

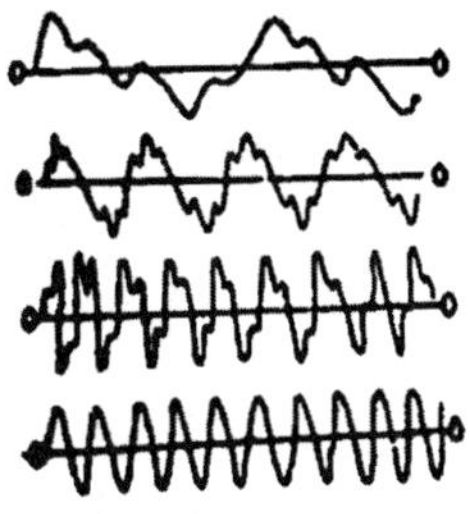

Fig. 59
Various patterns of wave shafts recording borrowed energy

The pair of spirals which wind light waves into spheres continue that winding until holes are bored through spheres and rings are formed, aided by the centrifugal force exerted by the expansion of the opposing spirals.

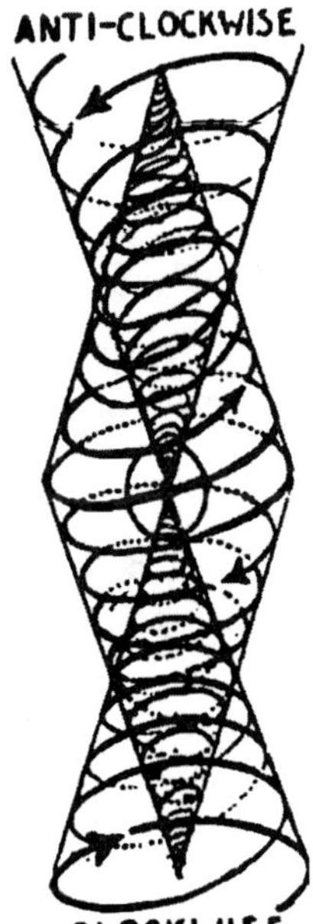

Fig. 60
Directions of spiral motion never reverses

Rings are the "death" half of the cycles of spheres. Rings recondense around points in space and rewind as spheres. The majestic ring nebula in Lyra (Fig. 61) is an outstanding example of the disintegration process of Nature. The ring exemplifies the "death" half of the cycle and the newly formed sun at its center the "life" half. A new body has been born out of the old one as it expanded into the heavens.

The heavens abound with new bodies appear-

Fig. 61
Lyra ring nebula

Fig. 62
Owl nebula

ing from old ones which have disappeared into another form. The Owl Nebula demonstrates this principle by two rings and two stars reborn from them. (Fig. 62)

The rings of Saturn will become moons, just as its other rings have become its several other moons. Our own moon was born from a ring from earth as it expands its bulk by absorbing its oceans, and accelerates its rotation as all of the outer planets have done. (Fig. 63)

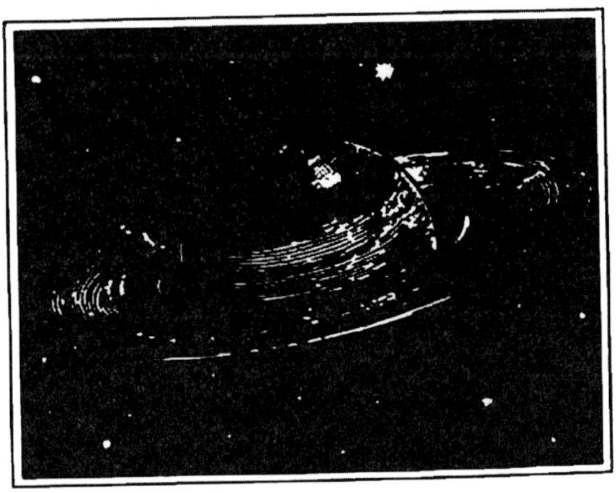

Fig. 63

Jupiter is even now developing belts which will be thrown off as rings, to become moons. These moons will become comets and eventually plunge into the sun as all things in this solar system likewise do.

Fig. 64 illustrates the unwinding process by means of which moons free themselves from the bindings of their mother shaft to again seek revolution around the shaft of their beginning in the sun.

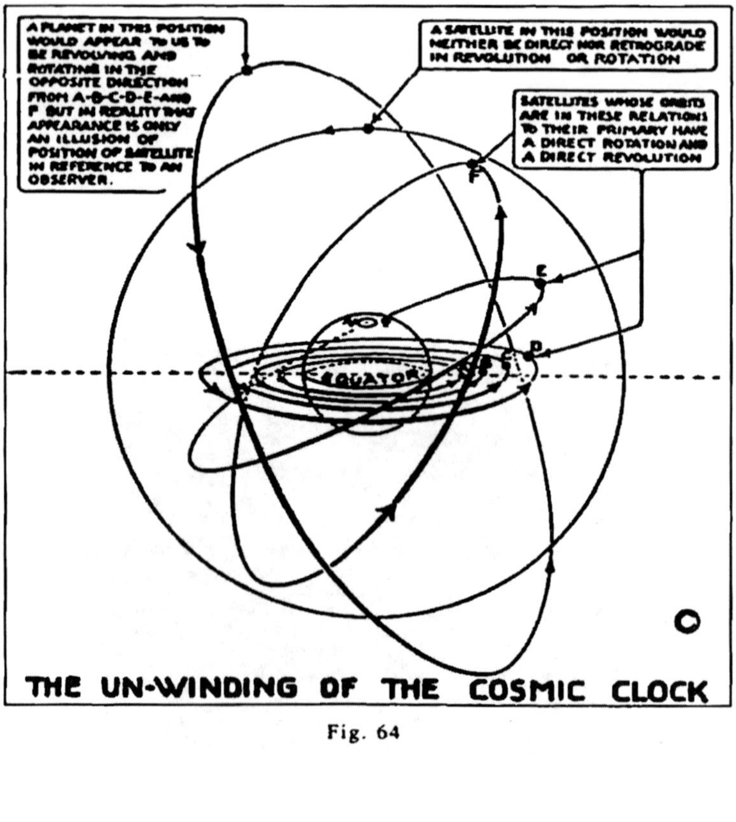

THE UN-WINDING OF THE COSMIC CLOCK

Fig. 64

Disintegration of suns and planets by radiation is accompanied by flattening at their poles. Spheres come into being by prolating and go out by oblating. Ever increasing speed of rotation around shafts is the cause of this phenomenon. Inner planets rotate very slowly upon their own shafts because they are so close to their mother shaft in the sun, but they revolve very swiftly in their orbits around the sun. (Fig. 65)

Mercury, our own moon, and Phobos, the inner moon of Mars, are so close to their mother shaft that they are obliged to revolve swiftly, with the same face always toward their primary. The outer planets have so far broken away from the influence of their mother shaft in the sun that their years have materially lengthened, their days conspicuously shortened, and their faces are constantly changing in relation to the sun.

Cyclones, waterspouts and tornadoes develop on our earth when spirals tighten around their shafts, for the

NATURE'S METHOD OF STORING ENERGY IN MASS

Fig. 38
As poles flatten equators lengthen

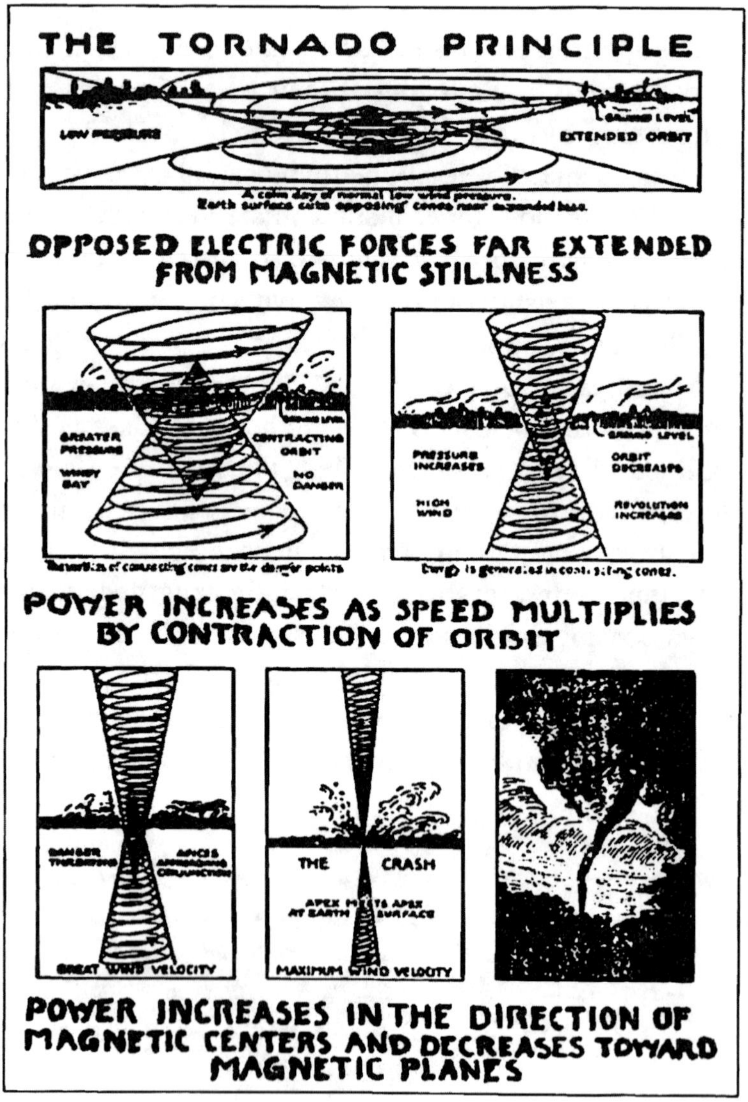
THE TORNADO PRINCIPLE
LOW PRESSURE
GROUND LEVEL
EXTENDED ORBIT
A calm day of normal low wind pressure.
Earth surface cuts opposing cones near expanded base.
OPPOSED ELECTRIC FORCES FAR EXTENDED FROM MAGNETIC STILLNESS
GREATER PRESSURE
WINDY DAY
GROUND LEVEL
CONTRACTING ORBIT
NO DANGER
PRESSURE INCREASES
HIGH WIND
GROUND LEVEL
ORBIT DECREASES
REVOLUTION INCREASES
Energy is generated in contracting cones.
POWER INCREASES AS SPEED MULTIPLIES BY CONTRACTION OF ORBIT
GREAT WIND VELOCITY
THE CRASH
APEX MEETS APEX AT EARTH SURFACE
MAXIMUM WIND VELOCITY
POWER INCREASES IN THE DIRECTION OF MAGNETIC CENTERS AND DECREASES TOWARD MAGNETIC PLANES

Fig. 66

more they thus contract, the greater their speed. When spirals are so wide at their bases that their angles to the earth's surface are negligible, there is calmness and peace; but when they contract to thin pencils which furiously speed around centering shafts of magnetic

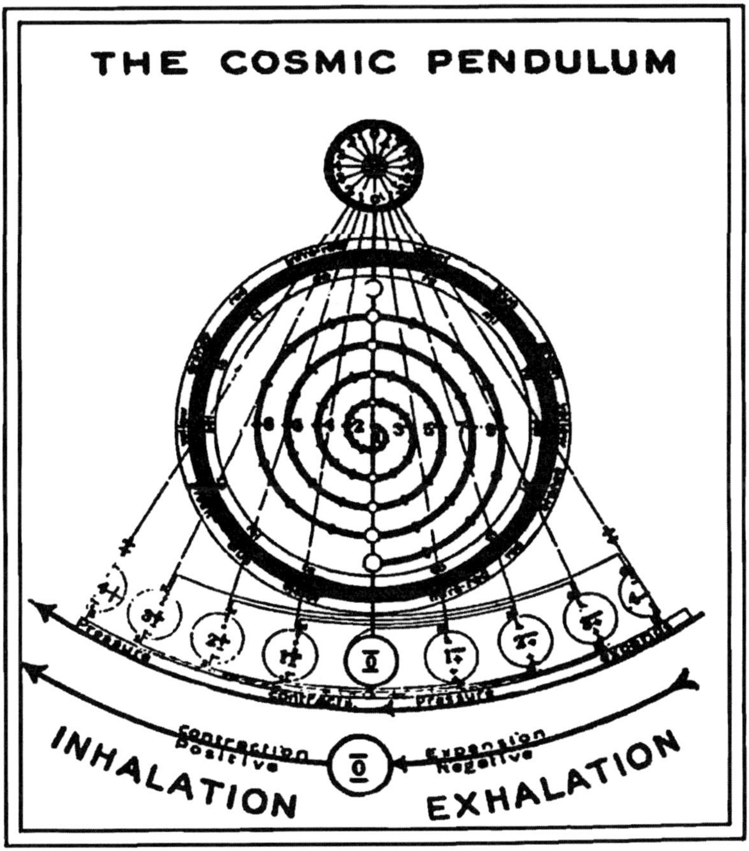

Fig. 67

stillness at ninety degrees to the earth's surface, they then do inestimable damage. (Fig. 66)

THE UNIVERSAL OCTAVE

The heartbeat of the universe, starting from zero of rest, spirals from its minimum to its maximum and back again to zero, in four pairs of opposite actions and reactions. These four pairs of opposite electric interweavers constitute the universal spiral octave wave by means of which the dynamic universe of *effect* rises from the static universe of *cause*. (Fig. 67)

The octave wave formula which governs all motion, and its birth position in the universal wave, is as follows in Fig. 68:

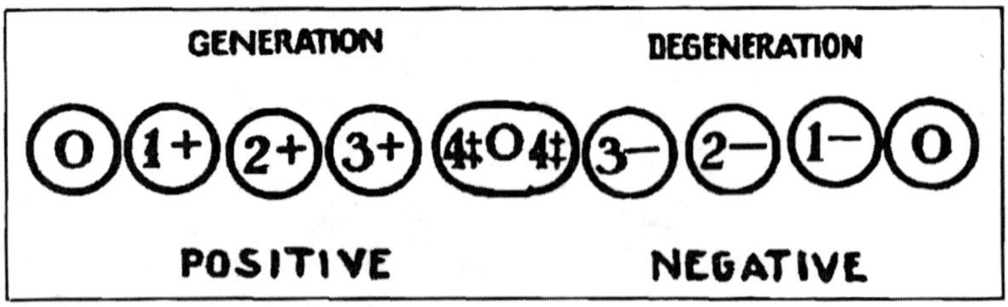

Fig. 68
Two-way journey from zero—through zero—to zero

Zero to four means the centripetal direction toward the apex of the spiral, which leads to higher potential, density, gravity and the white heat of incandescence. Four to zero means the centrifugal direction toward the base of the spiral which leads to lower pressure, lower potential, vacuity, radiativity and the black cold of space. Each of these is half of a cycle.

The reason an octave cannot be counted from one to eight, instead of from one to four, is because each of the pressures—which bear the relations of one to four positive in the octave—is a credit pressure, which has its equal opposite debit pressure in one to four negative.

The elements of matter, born on the spiral pairs of opposites as tones, have the same relation as tones of music have to the octave wave.

All wave motion is expressed in eight tones—four pairs of opposites. The middle pair is seemingly one. The octave is usually expressed as seven for this reason. An octave is a series of orderly harmonic tones. Tones are multiplied and divided pressures of light, spaced rhythmically with mathematical precision upon each octave wave of motion. The law which applies to one effect of motion applies to all, whether sound wave, electric current, color spectrum or octaves of elements of matter.

No state of motion has permanence or even duration. Everything is forever in a state of transition, changing its position in its wave by either multiplying or dividing its vibration frequencies to change its conditioning.

The basis of all octaves is the keynote of rest from which the octave springs to express the idea which lies within the magnetic stillness of that keynote. The fulcrum of the wave of musical octaves is its keynote from which all tonal changes in the octave are mathematically calculated in wave frequencies and volume. That keynote is always in one's consciousness whether the note is being sounded or not. It is the balance of its octave. All tones are out of balance with it at all times and forever desire balance. No state of motion can evade the keynote of rest from which it sprang, nor can it be separated from it electrically in matter—or consciously in Mind.

No matter what instrument produces octave tones, its frequencies and other dimensions must be in the orderliness demanded by the opening and closing spiral pairs which control those tones by conditioning them. Likewise, no matter what the instrument, whether larynx of man, string of violin, carbon wave field or color spectrum, its sole motivating power for producing change of dimension for the purpose of producing change of tone is electric pressure directed by desire and borrowed from the keynote of the octave's stillness. Furthermore, all power thus borrowed for one expression in any octave tone must be in balance with the opposite of that tone within which those borrowings have been debited.

This outstanding fact of natural law must be borne in mind in considering those principles as applied to the mechanics of the universal wave which produces the

Periodicity is a characteristic of all phenomena of nature

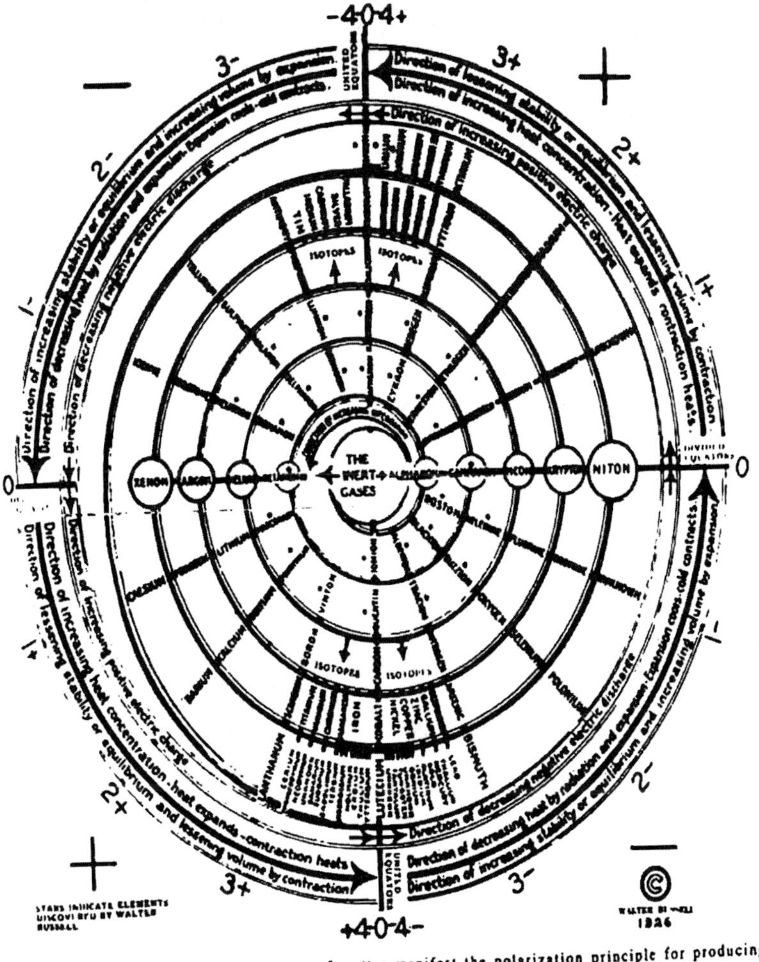

The nine octaves of the elements of matter manifest the polarization principle for producing dynamic action by extending two equators from a fulcrum point of rest. These two equators arise by gyroscopic action, multiplied centripetally, in four concentrative efforts to an amplitude plane which is 90 degrees from the zero plane of the inert gases. They then descend in four decentrative, depolarizing stages to disappear in their inert gases and again reappear from them in endless cycles throughout eternity. Thus do all bodies appear and disappear—to again reappear—forever.

Fig. 69

One of the two completed Mendeleef tables of the elements which Walter Russell gave to the world of science in 1926.

The Russell Periodic Table of the Elements

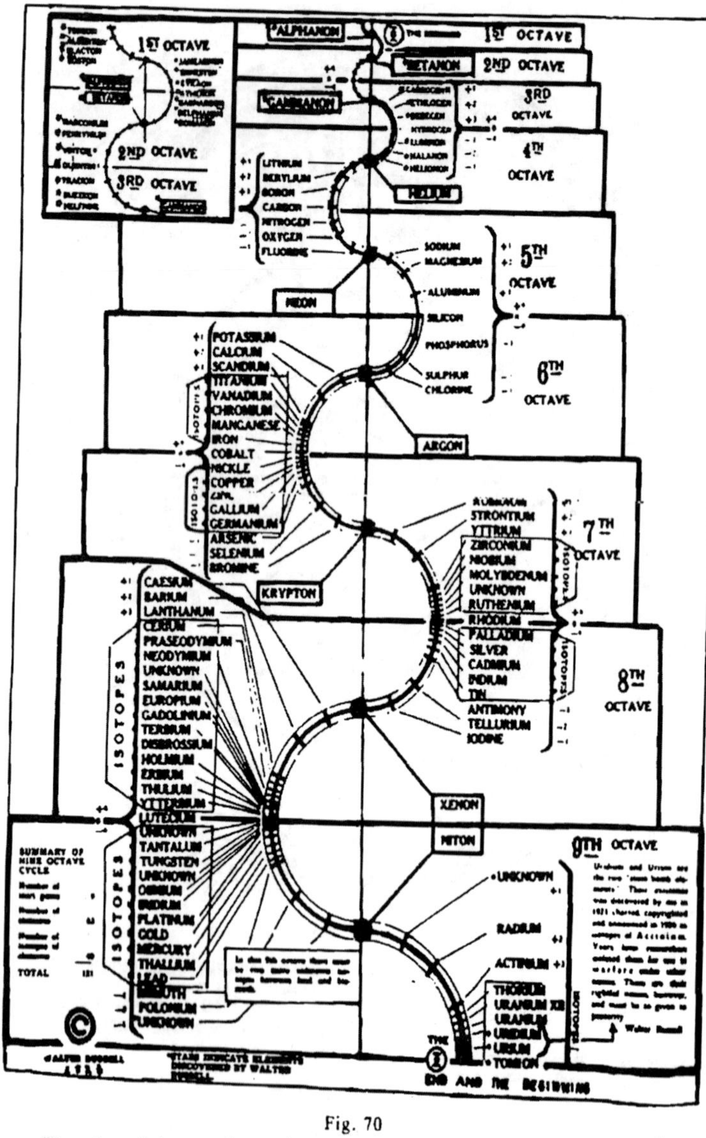

Fig. 70
The other of the two charts given to the world by Walter Russell in 1926.[4]

octave wave tones of the elements of matter with such precision that any effect produced by any of them in combination, or separately, will produce that same effect always.

THE ELEMENTS OF MATTER

An invariable characteristic of Nature is to express life-death cycles of any idea, in nine lesser interweaving cycles enfolded in the one. When we think of man as an

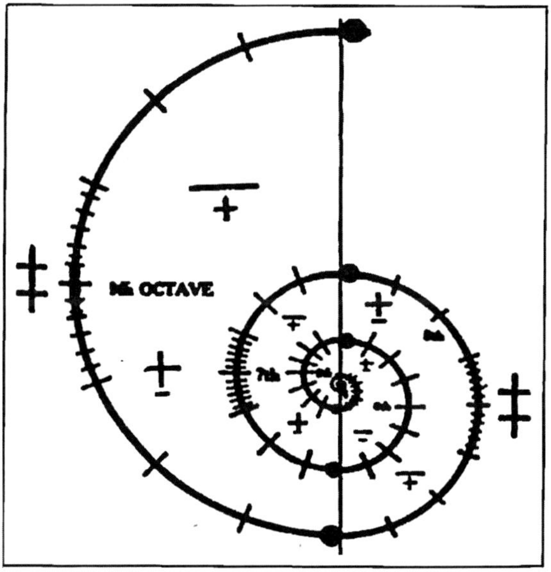

Fig. 71
The universal nine octave cycle

idea, we think of him as grown up to fullness of middle age. Until then, we think of generating man as infant, child and youth. Following his generating cycles come the degenerative ones in which he gradually repays all of his borrowings from his zero of rest and returns to that zero to again borrow power to re-express the idea of man. (Fig. 71)

This process of Nature, which expresses its cycles of idea in nine lesser cycles, is conspicuously present in the life-death cycles of the elements of matter. Carbon alone expresses the idea of matter. All the nine octaves of the elements are stages of unfoldment and refoldment of carbon. The first four and a half octaves lead to the maturity of carbon by the generative contraction of gravity. It is the hardest of all of the other stages of its transition, having the highest melting point. The last four and a half octaves lead from maturity through old age to disappearance at the end of the nine octave cycle by the radiative expansion of vacuity. (Fig. 70)

Genero-activity begins at the birth of carbon in the first octave with genero-active, inner explosive speed of light which is 186,400 miles per second. It ends with an equal radioactive, outer explosive speed. This speed is the limit at which motion can reproduce itself in curved wave fields before reaching zero where motion and curvature cease.

Carbon fulfills the plan of the Creator in His desire to

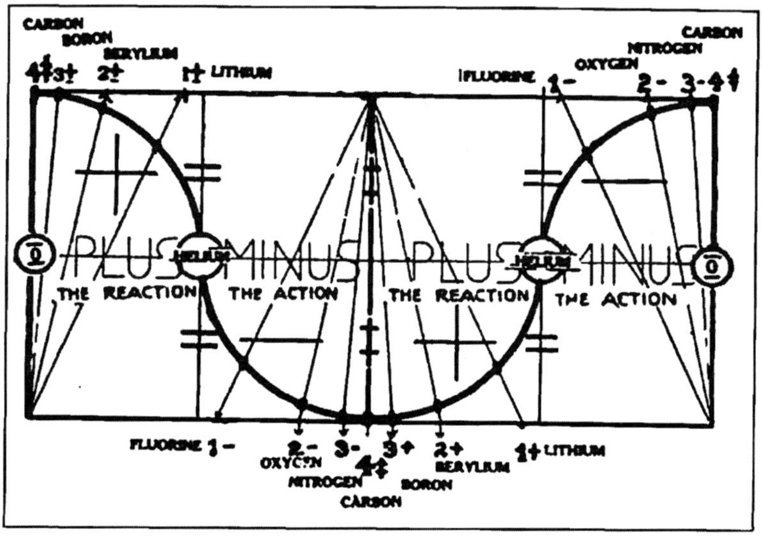

Fig. 72
Octave pressure relations

create but one form: the cube-sphere. Carbon alone crystallizes in true ćube, with all of the qualities of the true cube and sphere fully exemplified. All other elements which crystallize as cubes are octave extensions of carbon. All such extensions occupy the four-zero-four position of wave amplitude.

In carbon are all of the elements of its previous stages, just as in man are all of the actions and reactions of his previous stages. Hydrogen is a one octave younger prototype of carbon. It forms on the wave amplitude at four-zero-four just as carbon forms at four-zero-four one octave ahead. In hydrogen is a whole octave of elemental tones. Several of these have been recently discovered and wrongly named isotopes. Isotopes are split tones such as those which a violinist could produce between full tones.

An amazing thing happens at this point in the unfolding of carbon's life record. Hydrogen's melting point is 259 degrees below zero centigrade and in one octave the winding up process of nature acts like a whiplash at its halfway position where genero-activity and radioactivity meet as equals. This effect tightens the winding of carbon into such a dense substance that the melting point jumps to 3600 degrees above zero in that one octave.

Nature immediately counterbalances this accelerative action by dropping nitrogen, the next element beyond carbon, into a gas which melts at 210 degrees below zero centigrade. It does not recover from the gaseous condition during the rest of its octave.

The cosmic seed of the carbon octave is helium.

Silicon is one octave older than carbon. The melting point of silicon drops to less than one half of its younger stage: 1420 degrees.

The cosmic seed of the silicon octave is neon.

When carbon becomes still another octave older at the four-zero-four position of cobalt in the sixth octave, it divides its full tone into ten split isotope tones; five on either side. (Fig. 70)

Carbon at this stage has lost much of its vitality and changes its character by thus dividing it into cobalt isotopes. Its melting point has dropped to 1480 degrees, which is slightly higher than the silicon stage of carbon. Because of sharing that position with ten others it has lost much of its true cube-sphere quality of balance which the four-zero-four position manifests.

The evidence of that is the metallic quality of cobalt which would be impossible in the true cube-sphere position of four-zero-four in the octave wave.

The four-zero-four position is one of balance between the pairs of metallic opposites such as iron and nickel, manganese and copper, chromium and zinc or sodium and chlorine. When any of these pairs lose their metallic quality, such as iron and oxygen in iron rust, or sodium and chlorine in sodium-chloride, they find both rest and balance in the stony quality of the salts; they crystallize in the cubic system if they are equal or near equal opposite pairs. Sodium-chloride is a good example. One can see its approximately true cubes in sodium-chloride (ordinary table salt) or in the distorted cube crystals of sodium-iodide.

The four-zero-four position in the octaves of the elements is the position of rest where any action must end its half cycle and begin its other half. It comes to a point of rest before returning to a point of rest, as all actions and reactions in nature do.

At one octave of still further aging, carbon becomes rhodium and again climbs to its amplitude position at four-zero-four by five efforts and descends by five more. Rhodium is more vital than cobalt, for its melting point is 1950 degrees. (Fig. 70)

The cosmic seed of the rhodium octave is krypton.

Great vitality is often evidenced in Nature's creations

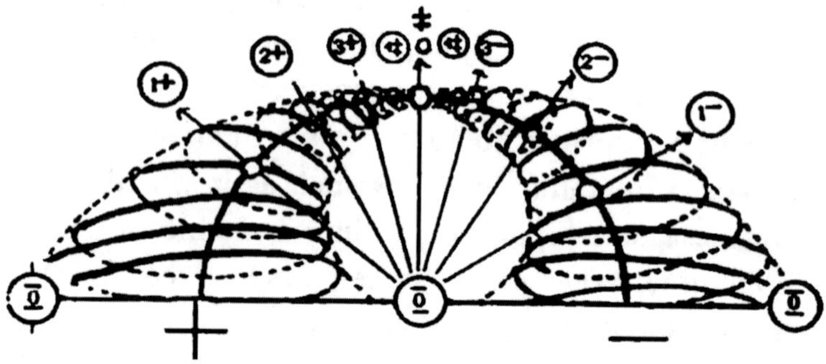

Fig. 73
Cycle of the elements from rest to rest

after they have fully matured. The radioactive death principle is as vital in disintegrating the body as the genero-active principle is in integrating it. That vitality is enhanced by the opposition of the genero-active resistance set up against it. Such strong, vital metals as silver, nickel, copper, tantalum, tungsten, osmium, platinum and gold belong to the aging half cycles of carbon.

Tantalum is a radioactive metal which becomes so dense because of opposition between the two electric conditioners that its melting point reaches 3400 degrees centigrade, or within two hundred degrees of carbon. Osmium follows with a melting point of 2700 degrees and platinum at 1755 degrees. In this octave, the violent drop from carbon's melting point to nitrogen's melting point at minus 210 is balanced by this corresponding genero-active reaction.

In the next octave of carbon's aging, the radioactive death principle becomes more evident in lutecium. After reaching its three position in the positive half of its octave, it arrives at its balance position of four-zero-four only after making thirteen efforts, as evidenced by thirteen isotopes including unknowns.[5] These are balanced by thirteen in the negative half cycle. Among these thirteen is the vital tungsten, a negative metal of great commercial value. By bombarding this metal with a sufficiently high current to cause it to disintegrate, it will discharge its seed of inert cosmic gases just as an oak tree will discharge its cosmic seed in acorns.

The cosmic seed of the lutecium octave is xenon.

The cosmic seed of carbon's last octave of disappearance arises from the inert gas niton.[6] Octaves unfold from their past recorded seed and they must have a seed into which their present record can refold. That principle is absolute in Nature.

Radium and actinium evidence the going-to-seed process of all completed cycles of growing things in a strong measure. One can see this process taking place in radium without resorting to the electrocution process referred to as applied to tungsten.

A small telescopic instrument, the spinthariscope, contains a needle upon which a microscopic portion of radium has been placed in front of a fluorescent screen. By looking through its lenses in the dark, one can see the shedding of the cosmic seed of the slowly dying carbon in its radium stage as the rays of those cosmic seeds bombard the screen. The effect is beautiful, like looking into the heavens on a starry night with all of its stars twinkling into appearance and disappearance as fireflies twinkle in the meadow on a dark night.

Carbon never comes within perception at tomium, but its efforts to reach tomium are evidenced in the uranium group of isotopes, of which there are fifteen before tomium is reached. Out of this group several have been found and made use of, especially those from which the atom bomb has been produced. (Fig. 70)

Radioactivity has so nearly reached its maximum at this point that the speed of the cosmic seed shed by these isotopes has been measured at 180,000 miles per second, which is approximately the speed of light nearing its ending point at tomion where the octave again begins at alphanon.

THE INERT GASES

The octaves of the elements of matter "grow" from seed, just as all things grow from seed. From the moment the elements unfold from their seed, they are in a constant state of transition, from the beginning of their cycle to the end. Elements are not fixed created *things*. They are pressure *conditions* of light waves. Those conditions of light pressures are constantly changing from infancy to old age in the elements of matter just as they are in the animal kingdom. The inert gases are cosmic elements which will not combine with any other elements. They constitute the recording system of this creating universe. They surround the zero from which motion springs and to which it returns. They represent minimum motion in the wave, just as amplitudes represent maximum motion. They are the seeds of the octaves of matter, and each octave has a different seed just as different trees have different seeds.

Elements are waves, and waves disappear and reappear. God's recording system does not allow any creating thing to disappear without recording the actions and reactions of its stages of appearance. All states of motion are recorded in the inert gases. In the inert gases are the souls of their bodily manifestations in the universe of motion. In them is desire for expression and the patterned form of that desire.

The cosmic inert gases fill all space between the stars of heaven. They insulate states of motion from each other by their balancing zero. They bring all motion into being through the will of the Creator, true to the pattern of desire. They are the source of balancing cosmic rays which interchange between zero and matter. They vitalize matter with the omnipotence of creative desire which lies within the zero of these cosmic rays.

There are nine cosmic gases; the first and the last being one. Alphanon begins the cycle and ends it. There is no beginning and no ending.

The list of cosmic gases follows: alphanon, betanon, gammanon, *helium, *neon, *argon, *krypton, *zenon, and *niton.[6]

SPECTRUM ANALYSIS

The known octaves which lie within the range of perception are five and one half. These begin with the third, or hydrogen octave, and end with the uranium group which are isotopes of actinium and tomium in the last octave.[7]

* Indicates those known.

The invisible octaves of finely divided matter of space are three and one half in number. These octaves are beyond our range of perception, but they are not beyond our knowing.[8]

Light is the universal language. Through spectrum analysis of light waves man has been able to analyze and recognize each element when in its incandescent stage.

By means of the spectroscope, he has been enabled to divide light rays through its prisms into the component parts which make up the life history of each stage of its two-way cycle.

Each element tells the story of its entire previous "incarnations" in other octaves, since its beginning. Any line in one octave is repeated in the next, but shifted in position because of the changing pressures of each succeeding octave.

The spectrum of hydrogen is preponderantly red. A bright red line indicates its present octave. Other red lines tell its past history in lower octaves.

The simple history of hydrogen, as compared to the complex spectrum of iron, is like the history of an obscure youth as compared to that of Napoleon.

In the spectrum analysis of iron, the lines which belong to iron and those which tell its recent and remote history can be seen at a glance. These lines also indicate the relative ability of the iron atom to charge or discharge.

Wave length 7181.8 is immediately recognizable as belonging to iron in its present octave; 6916.8 is recent history and 6944.8 is extremely remote history. Herein follows a partial list of lines whose wave lengths belong to iron or to its immediate mid-tone associates, and also other lists indicating its recent and its more remote history.[9]

BELONGING TO IRON	RECENT HISTORY	REMOTE HISTORY
7181.8	6916.8	6944.8
6495.1	6827.8	6678.1
6380.9	6335.4	6270.4
5905.8	6230.9	6232.8
5862.5	6157.9	6137.8
5859.8	6102.3	6027.2
5816.5	6003.2	6024.2
5658.9	5930.2	5983.1
5555.0	5701.7	5934.8
5041.9	5686.6	5662.7

The visible and invisible spectrum is divided into several thousand lines. Each line is different in its shade of color and in its plane. Each line proves that this universe of varying motion is a universe of varying pressures.

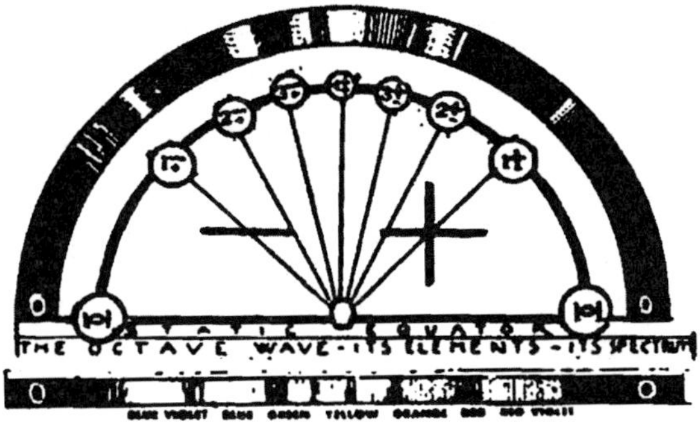

Fig. 74
Relation of tones of the elements to tones of the spectrum

ATOMIC STRUCTURE

The elements of matter are not different substances or different things. They are different pressure conditions of light waves. The light units of the elements are all alike but are differently conditioned by the electric pressures exerted upon them during the inward or outward spiral journey from zero to zero.

The unanswered mystery of how the elements become mathematically precise octave tones, just as musical tones or color tones of the spectrum are mathematically precise in vibration orderliness, lies in the wave field gyroscopic principle.

Together the eight elements of an octave form two halves of one whole cycle of tones which ascend from zero to the four-zero-four position of amplitude and then descend again to zero to begin anew.

This spiral journey contracts into greater pressures as it approaches wave field amplitude positions at spiral apices, and expands into lower ones on the return journey to spiral bases.

That two-way spiral journey of each half cycle extends between six mirrors of still Light which compose the wave field, and winds around a still shaft which

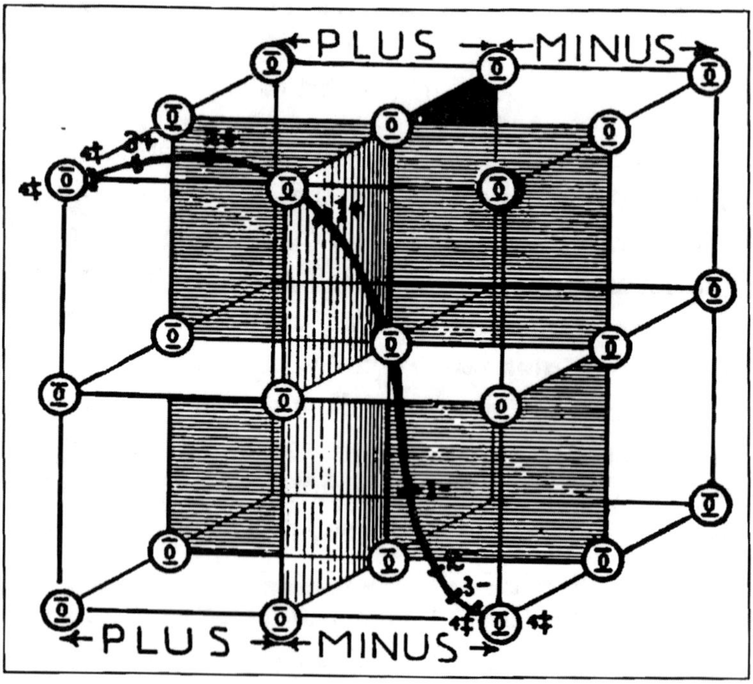

Fig. 75
Locations of elements on wave fields are determined by wave-field mirrors

centers the spiral. Three of these mirrors are the mirrors of action and three are the mirrors of reaction. (Fig. 75)

The three of action are the inner intersection planes of the cube and the three of reaction are the outer boundary planes of the wave field.

All of these planes of the wave field are of zero curvature, but the spiral universe which is forming within those planes is curved. Curved planes of light act as two-way lenses which bend light to focal points and extend it from those focal points radially.

As the two-way spirals of forming matter extend from the wave field center in opposite directions toward wave field intersections, the six mirror planes of still light focus three points of still light upon the still shaft of each half cycle. Centers are formed at these focal points which become the one, two, three positive and negative elements of matter by rotating gyroscopically upon the wheels of light which act as equators for those borning tones.

Multiplying and dividing pressures determine the density and volume of each succeeding element. The color spectrum records these pressures as the complete history of every element from octave to octave of the whole nine octave cycle of the elements.

Multiplying pressures of the spiral also affect the curvature of its light lenses to such an extent that the focusing positions change their mathematical ratios in conformity with the acceleration of gravity and the deceleration of radiation.

The positions of focal centers of gyroscopic wheels upon the wave shaft are thus affected as diagrammed in Fig. 76 and Fig. 72. Each element is the square of

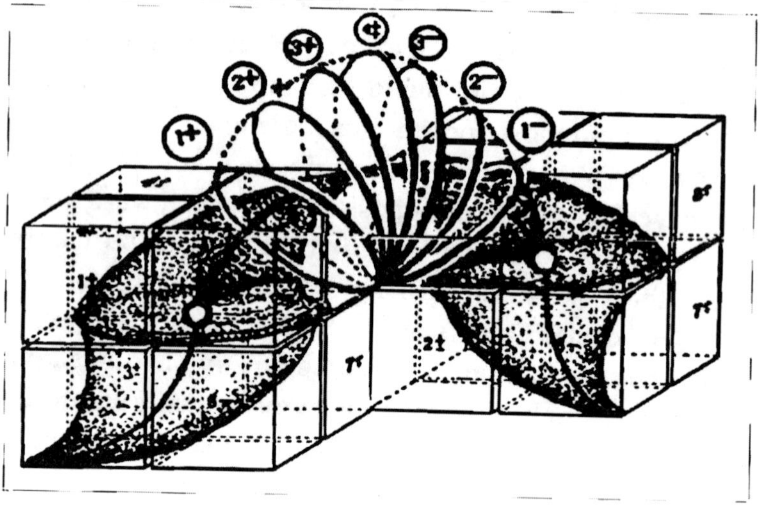

Fig. 76
The octave gyroscopic principle

the distance to and from its succeeding one, in accordance with its direction. The direction of gravity is the inverse square, and the opposite direction is the direct square.

The volume of each succeeding element is likewise affected directly and inversely as the cube.

Six of the eight gyroscopic wheels of the whole octave are thus accounted for by geometric projection of two-way opposed lights through each other, from two sets of three mirror boundary fields. The fourth double tone is formed at the rest point where eight cube wave fields meet. This is the point of rest which is known as the center of gravity in earths or suns—where motion and curvature cease.

The completed sphere thus becomes a section of eight adjoining wave fields and revolves around that point of rest upon the wave shaft where the two half cycles of the wave meet.

For this reason the four-zero-four position is one of balance in which the yellow of orange is the dominating color of one of its two gyroscopic wheels and the yellow of green is the other, centered by white.

At the two points upon the still shaft of the turning sphere where the shaft penetrates its surface are the magnetic poles of still Light which control the balance of each sphere's turning. One of these is the north magnetic pole which controls the winding of the sphere into density by centripetal electric force, and the other is the south magnetic pole which controls its unwinding centrifugally into space.[10]

In a sphere such as our nearly mature sun, these magnetic poles are practically upon the sun's pole of rotation, but upon oblating planets, such as our earth, the magnetic poles are removed from that pole of rotation in accordance with the measure of the earth's oblateness.

The elements of matter are miniature stellar systems. Every principle and law which applies to one applies to the other. This solar system is a gyroscopic wheel in the position which iron occupies in the elemental series. When it spirals a little further it will correspond to a carbon atom.[11] The sun will then be a true sphere and its new planets will also be true spheres.

The gyroscopic principle accounts for that law of Nature which causes like elements to seek each other. All decomposing compounds are sorted out, element by element, gyroscopically.

The efforts of man to transmute one element into another must be governed by this principle, and not upon the theory that another substance will be obtained by "knocking out one electron." It makes no difference how many planets there are in a solar or atomic system in so far as its "substance" as an element is concerned. One or more added or subtracted would not change the element into another substance any more than one or more children would affect the nationality of their parents.

Transmutation will become simplified by observing that the plane of gyration, in relation to amplitude, and the speed of revolution of the gyroscopic wheel upon its still shaft, will alone change volume by either multiplying or dividing density.

Great possibilities in new metals lie in the proper application of this principle.

THE SHAPE OF THE UNIVERSE

This ageless universe *has* no shape. It has a seeming infinite extension, but that extension is a reflected one. This electric universe of two-way extended light is but a series of mirrors which reflect into each other through curved lenses. Its seeming extension might be likened to a light within a mirror-bound room.

One light within such a mirrored enclosure would seemingly extend infinitely, but the light thus mirrored would be the same light. The reflected extension would have no reality.

The idea of continuity or discontinuity is based upon mirrored effect of an initial Cause. Continuity infers time. Time is but one of the effects which constitutes this universe. Time flows two ways, but the senses detect only the forward flow. They cannot detect the backward flow which cancels out the forward flow. Time is as unreal as the wave universe is unreal.

What is true in principle of one wave is true of all waves. Each wave is a two-way reflected extension of an equilibrium zero which we call a vibration. Vibrations appear, disappear and reappear from their source of rest to manifest idea which is existent alone in rest. Just as the vibration of one wave disappears into its zero of universal stillness, so do all vibrations disappear into the universal zero of stillness. This zero universe of vibrating waves can have no shape other than a seeming one.

THE VOIDING PRINCIPLE

This is a zero universe of seeming mechanical motion of force exerted in a seeming three-dimensional universe.

Every action of any nature begins with zero, counts up to nine, to end and begin again at zero. Beyond nine it cannot go, but up to nine it must go. Nine is universal.

Nine is universal because it is the wave field number—the eight of the cube centered by the zero of gravity in the sphere.

Our decimal system is based upon the wave field of the cube sphere. It is as follows:

	0 -	1 -	2 -	3 -	4 -	0 -	4 -	3 -	2 -	1 -	0
equals	10 -	1 -	2 -	3 -	4 -	5 -	6 -	7 -	8 -	9 -	10

The musical scale and the spectrum of Nature correspond to the wave field tones. They are as follows:

musical	0 -	1 -	2 -	3 -	4 -	0 -	4 -	3 -	2 -	1 -	0
tones	do -	re -	mi -	fa -	sol -	rest -	sol -	fa -	mi -	re -	do
	(Keynote)					(Overtone)					(Keynote)
spectrum	black	red	red	orange	yellow	white	yellow	green	blue	blue	black
tones		violet								violet	

Fig. 75 demonstrates this fact. The three centering planes are centered by zero. All intersections of these planes add up to eight. Eight, centered by their zero source, equals nine. Likewise the cube itself adds up to eight by counting the intersections of its six faces. Also there are eight directions of action and eight of reaction; each eight being four pairs, which are nine by adding the centering zero.

Nine is the three times three of length, breadth and height extended from zero. The length, breadth and height of any expression is two extended zeros centered by zero. (Fig. 2, p. 219)

Length and breadth are static, for they are both on equipotential levels. Height is dynamic, for it is radial.

The universal nine of matter and space is three mirrors of rest, centered by rest, from which all three extend at right angles to each other, each mirroring itself into the other. (Fig. 75)

The universal nine of the octave is four pairs of opposite pressures extending diagonally from zero which centers the cube to eight zeros which corner the cube. (Fig. 75)

The measure of extension from zero to zero is desire for extension. Desire for extension from zero to zero is energy in zero. Energy extended from zero to zero is manifested by pressures of desire equally multiplied and divided—equally added and subtracted

—equally credited and debited—and equally and oppositely conditioned. The sum of all these balanced effects is zero. (Fig. 75)

Zero pressures equally multiplied and divided are manifested by the action and reaction of motion. Motion is a projection of the opposed energy pressures of desire from within a centering zero to the extended mirrors of rest, which measure desire and mirror it back to rest in the centering zero as expressed desire. The sum of dually reflected motion thus expressed is zero.

Zero thus extended by action to fulfill desire for expression, and simultaneously mirrored back to manifest the fulfillment of expressed desire, is all there is to this universe of rest. Zero multiplied or divided—added or subtracted—extended or retracted —results in zero. This is a zero universe in all effects of motion—a seeming universe in time and sequence —and a mirage universe of imagined form.

It is a universe of two negations which simultaneously cancel each other and sequentially repeat the cancelling of their negations to create the illusion that zero can be multiplied—or divided—or added to —or subtracted from—to create a reality which never is nor can become. (Fig. 75)

That is what Creation is. It is the imagining of knowing. Knowing is Light. Light is still. Imagining is thinking.

Thinking is the imagined action and reaction of motion mirrored from zero of rest to zero of rest.

This is a still universe of the Light of knowing. In it is no activity.

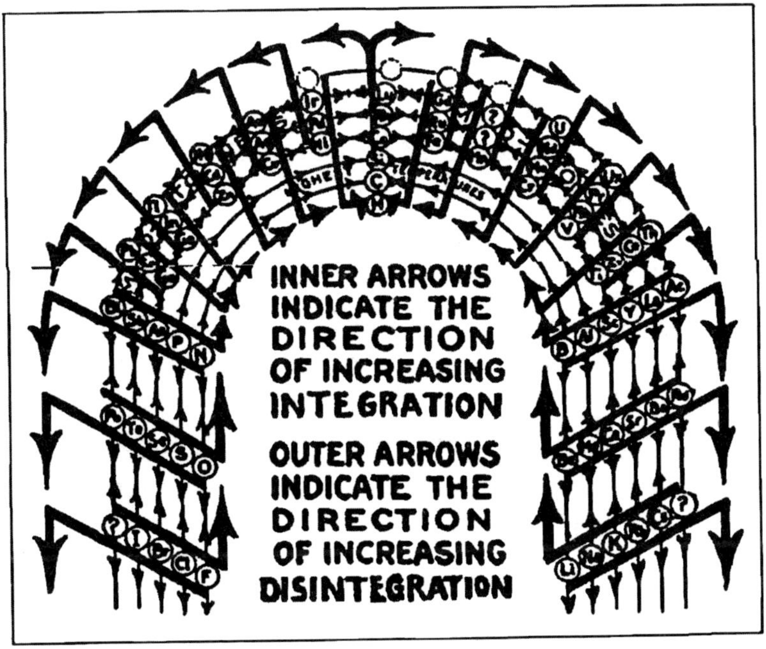

Fig. 77
Opposite actions simultaneously void each other

But what about our senses? Our senses tell us otherwise. Our senses are inadequate. They deceive us mightily. And that is good, else the play of Creation could not be played. The senses record but little of the whole. If the senses could but see the whole there would be no play. The senses record motion alone for the senses themselves are but motion. Motion is an illusion which only *seems*. It has no being.

The senses do not *know*, but man believes that his senses *do know*—and in that belief lies man's confusion.

The senses, being but motion, sense moving things and moving light mirrored as moving things. They sense the forward movement of an airplane piling up compression ahead of it—but they do not record the mirrored invisible counterpart of that plane—equal to it in potential and speed—moving backward into a vacuum behind the plane which simultaneously voids the compression ahead of it.

This inadequacy of the senses to record the backward flow of forward moving things—causes the illusions of sequence and of time.

In Fig. 77 this principle, diagrammed by arrows extending two ways from every element in the whole known series, indicates that integration is simultaneously balanced by disintegration. No time interval elapses between the debiting of any credit extended to opposites in Nature.

Fig. 78 diagrams all matter as pairs of opposite conditions. Each line is connected with its opposite mate. Each of the pair is a negation of the other one. Each pair

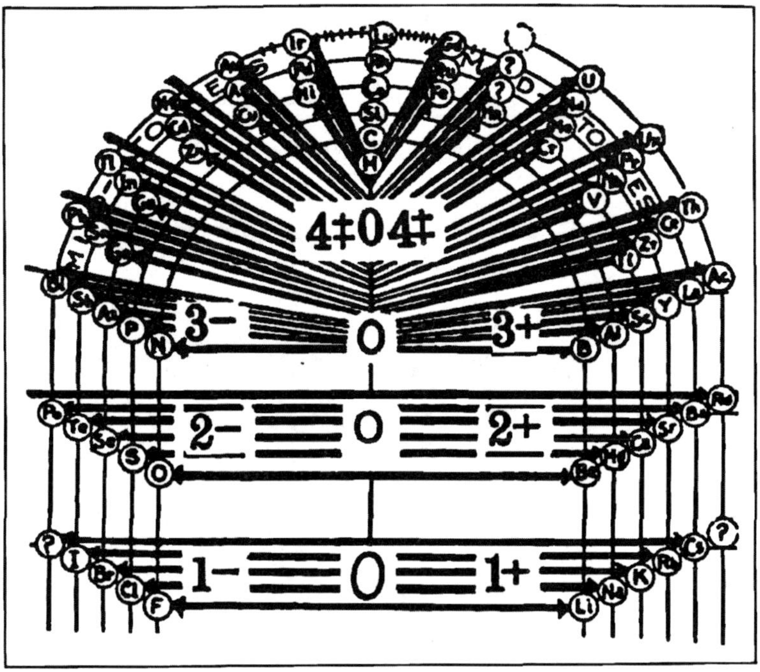

Fig. 78
This universe of matter is composed of pairs of negations which never exceed zero

is conditioned as the two tanks of air in Fig. 18 and the storage battery in Fig. 19, on page 231, are conditioned. Each one of these elemental pairs is an equal and opposite mirrored extension from a centering zero fulcrum.

The fulcrum of all effect is the One Light of God.

GOD ALONE IS—IN MAN—AND IN ALL THINGS

"Every action is voided as it occurs, is repeated as it is voided, and recorded as it is repeated."

—*From* THE DIVINE ILIAD

1. Walter Russell shows here that sensed observation can result in incomplete vision and incomplete scientific laws. He points out that Newton based his law of gravitation on his observation of what gravity did to an apple, while admitting he did not know what gravity was. Newton did not sense the whole cycle of the apple in time "falling" up to the heavens as it disintegrates and reverses potential.

   Walter Russell states that Newton's mathematical formulae, written to prove that the moon would fall into the earth if its motion were stopped, applies to "every satellite, planet and star in the heavens, as well as to every electron in every atom, none of which are falling into their primaries." Walter Russell implies that Newton's laws of gravitation were incomplete. It is obvious from the Russell cosmogony that the moon can never stop its motion, nor can any of the other bodies that move around their primaries stop moving. They do not fall because they are always seeking and finding, losing and refinding their potential positions in their movements. If they were to stop their motion, they and all the Universe would disappear. If they were to stop their orbital motion and move inward or outward, to or from their primary, there would be a counterbalancing movement from their primary to balance this change of pattern unto the furthermost reaches of the Universe.

   In *A New Concept of the Universe* (pp. 50-52), Walter Russell takes up this subject again. He says that Newton concluded the moon has weight in relation to the earth similar to how a cannon ball has weight to the earth. This assumes that the moon had to have an "initial impulse" to keep it rotating around the earth to keep it from falling into it. Russell concluded that Newton's belief that weight is a fixed property of matter instead of an ever changing property of ever changing polarity was the result of sensed observation. See reference to this note on page 46 in this third edition of *The Secret of Light*.

2. Walter Russell in all of his later writings spoke of gravity as being a thrusting inward from without. For example, in *Atomic Suicide?* this concept is expressed in various ways, as on page 134: "Bear in mind the fact that you are compressing from the outside inward," and on page 135, "There is no force of any nature which holds it together by an inward pull. Nature does not attract nor does it repel. It compresses within a vacuum." He also expresses this idea on pages 89, 104-105, 138-139, and 145. In the *Home Study Course* this idea is expressed on page 719: "The word 'magnetism' is also unjustifiable. The word GRAVITY should be used instead, for gravity both multiplies and divides by thrusting inward from without to compress and outward from within to expand." This viewpoint is explored in considerable detail on pages 719, 724-727, and 733-735 of the *Home Study Course*.

   On page 10 of *A New Concept Of The Universe* Russell says, "One of these two electric conditions thrusts inward toward a center to create a centripetal vortice to simulate gravity. On the other side of the dividing equator, the other condition thrusts outward from a center to create a centrifugal vortice to simulate vacuity." On page 40 the idea is expressed as, "An outward explosion compresses in advance of the direction of the action and *simultaneously* evacuates in the opposite direction. The following half of the cycle is in reverse. The evacuated condition becomes a compressed one, and the compressed condition becomes an evacuated one." This idea is expressed directly and implied in many other pages throughout *A New Concept Of The Universe*. See references to this note on pages 149, 185, 189, 226, and 227 in this edition of *The Secret of Light*.

3. All motion—whether electric, light wave, or any kind of motion—always occurs between a cathode and an anode. Movement from cathode to anode occurs in an inward bound, centripetally directed manner towards more density and greater mass at the anode. All motion in this direction is compressive and contracting. Movement from anode to cathode occurs in an outward bound, centrifugally directed manner towards greater tenuity at the cathode. All motion from anode to cathode is extensive and expanding. Reference to this note appears on page 167.

4. Editors' note regarding the nine octave periodic chart (as of 1994.) There were elements predicted by Walter Russell as unknowns in his 1926 charts that were discovered prior to this date that he was unaware of. These elements, their discovery dates and octave positions are: Hafnium (1923) in the eighth octave at the third locking point, thirteenth isotopic position on the blue spectral side; and Rhenium (1925) in the eighth octave, third locking point, tenth isotopic position on the blue spectral side.

   Protactinium was discovered in 1917 and Walter Russell named this as Uranium XII in his 1926 charts. This element occurs in the ninth octave, third locking point, second isotopic position on the red spectral side.

   There were elements predicted by Walter Russell in his 1926 charts that were subsequently discovered after 1926 and before publication of *The Secret Of Light* in 1947 whose discovery at that time he was still unaware of. These elements, their dates of discovery and octave positions are: Technetium (1937), seventh octave, third locking point, fourth isotopic position on the red spectral side; Francium (1939), ninth octave, first locking point, on the red spectral side; and Astatine (1940), eighth octave wave, first locking point on the blue spectral side.

   Note that each octave runs from inert gas keynote to the next inert gas keynote with the amplitude element at the center of each octave. For instance, gammanon is the keynote for the hydrogen octave with hydrogen as the amplitude element, so the octave runs from gammanon through carbogen and helionon to helium as the next carbon octaves keynote. The octaves are designated by the vertical brackets to the sides of the element names and the amplitude elements are designated by their names and the horizontal lines running through these amplitude positions. Reference to this note appears on page 262.

5. There are thirteen isotopes, if you consider and count the unknown element between neodymium and samarium on the positive or male, red half of the cycle; and there are thirteen isotopes on the negative or female, blue half of the cycle counting the two unknown isotopes between lutecium and tantalum and between tungsten and osmium and if you also count two more isotopes that Walter Russell says in a note at the right side of these isotopes must exist between lead and bismuth. See reference to this note on page 269.

6. Niton, discovered in 1908, is now known as radon. See pages 269 and 272.

7. The visible octaves may be considered to be five and one half in number if one ignores the three known elements of the third octave; and the unknown and invisible elements of the last half of the ninth octave. The last half of the ninth octave is considered to be part of the first, invisible, space octaves. It precedes the first full octave which begins with the keynote inert gas alphanon. See page 272.

8. The invisible space octaves beyond our range of present perception may be considered three and one half in number: if one considers 1) the last half of the ninth octave to be part of the first, invisible, space octaves, and 2) all of the third octave elements to be unknown, though only four elements are yet undiscovered. The last half of the ninth octave includes the elements tomion, alberton, blacton, and boston. The four yet unknown elements of the third octave are carbogen, luminon, halanon, and helionon. The three known elements of this octave are hydrogen, ethlogen (deuterium) and bebegen (tritium.) See page 273.

9. Walter Russell's reference source for the spectral lines for iron came from *An introduction To The Study Of Spectral Analysis* in the Catalogue of Spectra, pages 185-206. Authored by W. Marshall Watts D.Sc., B.Sc. F.I.C., published in 1904 by Longmans Green and Company, London, and printed by William Glowes And Sons, Limited, London. Present scientific texts have different standards and different spectral readings for iron. See reference to this note on page 274 of this book.

10. In all other places in his works, Walter Russell speaks of the north and south magnetic poles as both being charging poles that wind the sphere into density by centripetal force. He also later removed the term magnetism in relation to what we normally call the magnetic field, saying that this too was electric motion. On page 30 of *A New Concept of the Universe* Russell says, "Radiation is an electric effect. It is not magnetic." And again on the same page he says, "There are no magnetic lines

of force in Nature." The term magnetism was reserved for the "stillness" of the "Zero universe of mind knowing."

On page 27 of *A New Concept of the Universe* Russell says, "These two points of stillness where electric motion reverses from one opposite pressure condition to the other are what science calls magnetic poles. The office of magnetic poles is to balance and control all electrically-divided motion in the universe. ... All electrically-divided matter, ... is controlled by a still centering point of magnetic light." In this view all effects that science normally calls electric and magnetic he chose to call electric.

This corresponded to his change in describing gravity. He also named electricity and gravity as One. He called gravity both the inward and the outward directed electric motion, saying it was a thrusting inward from without and a thrusting outward from within. See note number one.

In this way he unifies what is normally called gravity, radiation, electricity and magnetism as the same entity or process. In one phase it is inward bound, compressing, heating, charging and contracting; in the other it is outward bound, extending, cooling, discharging, and expanding. On page 715 of the *Home Study Course* , the Russells say, "Creation must henceforth be looked upon as AN OPTICAL UNIVERSE OF GRAVITY CONTROLLED LIGHT..."

On page 31 of *A New Concept of the Universe* he says, "The curvature of gravitation is centripetal. It is controlled by the north-south magnetic poles." And, on the same page he continues with, "The system of radial curvature is centrifugal. It is controlled by two as-yet-unknown magnetic poles which will amply be described later as east-west poles."

Therefore, we could rewrite the sentences this note refers to on page 279 of *The Secret Of Light* as follows: At the two points upon the still shaft of the turning sphere where the shaft penetrates its surface are the north-south magnetic poles of still Light, which along with the east-west equipotential circumferential poles of still magnetic Light, control the balance of the sphere's turning. The north-south magnetic poles control the winding of the sphere into density by centripetally directed generative, electric force of gravity, and the east-west poles control its unwinding by the centrifugally directed radiative, electric force of gravity."

In this way the statement conforms to his later vision of how he termed magnetism, radiation, and generation: Magnetism resides in the stillness of the zero point center of the pole-shaft (the still magnetic Light of Mind); radiation exhibits the outward electric thrust of gravity; and generation exhibits the inward electric thrust of gravity. Reference to this note appears on page 279.

11. After spiraling further, iron will correspond to a cobalt atom in the carbon amplitude position. See page 280.

INDEX

INDEX

M

T

U